MASTERING PRANAYAMA

MASTERING PRANAYAMA

From Breathing Techniques to Kundalini Awakening

Radhika Shah Grouven

THATfirst Publishing
Germany 2018

MASTERING PRANAYAMA

Cover Design: Olivier D.
Book Design: Kai Rübsamen
Author Photo: Jèrôme Gravenstein

P–ISBN: 978-3-947389-01-8
E–ISBN: 978-3-947389-00-1

Published by THATfirst Publishing 2018
www.that-first.com

Dedicated, in Deepest Gratitude,
To My Mother

ACKNOWLEDGEMENT

I would like to express gratitude to the many teachers of the Oral Tradition who have been custodians of this knowledge over millennia. Among these, one distinguished name stands apart: Swami Rama. A veritable fountain of wisdom, Swami Rama has been a great source of inspiration for this book.

I would like to thank Joachim for all the time, effort and resourcefulness that has gone into creating the excellent illustrations and tables throughout the book. Many thanks also to Miklos for proofreading the book.

CONTENTS

Part 2: Advanced

CHAPTER SUMMARIES

Part 1: The Foundation

Chapter 1: Pranayama, the Shortcut to Immortality
Pranayama, the ancient Science of Life challenges our preconceived notions of death and life and takes us on an incredible journey, where the impossible becomes possible.

Chapter 2: Are you breathing right?
No one ever asked you this question before and you never thought about it. Unfortunately it is true: most of us do not know how to breathe right. Lesson one is unlearning wrong breathing habits.

Chapter 3: Finding the Best Posture or the Science of Sitting
With seven postures to choose from, sitting is not just sitting. Lesson two is finding the right posture and preparing a comfortable seat. It may not look like it, but this is one of the most challenging stages of the journey. Don't give up before you have really started.

Chapter 4: Basic Breathing Techniques
Having overcome the initial obstacles, finally you start practicing real breathing techniques only to discover: they are not so basic after all. These practices will take you from fifteen breaths per minute to one breath per minute. If you achieve this in less than a year, you have every reason to congratulate yourself.

Chapter 5: Svarodaya, the Mystical Science of Breath
Learning to churn up the subtle energy and integrating it requires one-pointedness. The feminine and masculine energies are harmonized; the divided mind and body are brought into balance. Practice regularly and you are well on your way to become a master of the fine breath and even finer mind.

Part 2: Advanced

Chapter 6: An Ancient Secret is revealed
You always wanted to be in on a secret? That moment has arrived. A word of caution though: the difficulty lies not in the ability to practice the secret, but in the ability to accept it. Accept that it is possible and you will be soon saying, "Look, no hands!" Then you can tell one and all that you are an advanced practitioner.

Chapter 7: The Wedding of the Sun and the Moon
Twilight moments have kept mystics and poets busy since a long time, and not without reason. Twilight is that mystical moment when the mind is naturally contemplative. As you stand at the threshold of the inner world, the question you need to ask yourself is: "Do I really want to be an adept?"

Chapter 8: Holding on to the Thread of Awareness
Life is a wondrous rainbow. As you transition from one color to another, you discover, there are no compartments, no divisions; just beautiful shades that flow into each other. Awareness is the thread that takes you through the transitions of life as well as death.

Chapter 9: The Importance of Lifestyle or How to enjoy Life
Life has so much to offer, but there is such a thing as "too much of a good thing." Do not be afraid of discipline. Discipline is your friend. Enjoy life with complete awareness and you will soon notice that even the coffee tastes much better.

Chapter 10: Kumbhaka, the Elusive Breathless State
Breathlessness should lead to eternal life? Paradoxes like this will challenge your world view, and hopefully even destroy it. Plunge into this deep and vibrant silence, one you have never known before and you will long to return to it. The longing will lead you.

Chapter 11: The Mysterious Fourth Pranayama
After uninterrupted practice over a long period of time something odd happens. It seems, all the practices start merging and lead to one and the same place, a place of reasonless joy and profound beauty. The fourth pranayama is the direct experience of prana itself.

Chapter 12: Reversal of Subtle Energy or Kundalini Awakening
Are you upside down? Or is the world topsy turvy? The death of ignorance is the birth of wisdom. An adept, a mystic, a seer is born. All the same, awakening the kundalini is not the same as leading it consciously.

Chapter 13: Leading Kundalini
In any other book, this would be the end, but in this book, it is a new beginning. The harnessed kundalini brings with it the unlimited power of the deep unconscious and the knowledge of life, the world and everything.

PREFACE

"Lead me from ignorance to Truth.
Lead me from darkness to Light.
Lead me from death to Immortality.
Om shanti, shanti, shanti."

Brihadaranyaka Upanishad I.iii.28

In the last few decades, there has been a tremendous interest in yogic practices. However, the interest has been limited to asanas or physical postures, and there are few authoritative works on the subject of pranayama.

The teachings and practices elaborated in this book draw upon the Oral Tradition, based on empirical observations over thousands of years, handed down and validated by every following generation. This came to be known as the Oral Tradition since most of these teachings and practices were not recorded for many generations. Even though much was subsequently documented, the core teachings and the complementary practices were, and are to this day, only handed down step by step and accompanied by personal instructions. A great deal of effort has been made to maintain the authenticity and purity of these traditional teachings and practices, which cannot be compared with those taught by modern schools of physical culture.

Since the Oral Tradition predates the modern way of life by many millennia, an effort has been made to draw parallels between the traditional science of pranayama and modern science. While this may help the modern reader to relate to the traditional science, this book is not based on modern science or medicine; its focus remains the teachings and practices of the Oral Tradition.

As you systematically go through these practices, you may make many interesting observations and come across some difficulties. I have used illustrations and tables extensively to avoid misunderstandings. All the same, a book has its limitations and cannot be a substitute for personal guidance. Over the last two decades of teaching in the traditional way, I have grown to appreciate the wisdom of the Oral Tradition with its emphasis on direct dialogue with the student. There seems to be no other way to impart the higher secrets.

Radhika Shah Grouven

MASTERING PRANAYAMA

Part 1: The Foundation

"Still others offer as sacrifice the outgoing breath into the incoming breath, while some offer the incoming breath into the outgoing breath, seizing the movement of the outgoing and incoming breaths, intent upon the mastery of the life force."

Bhagavad Gita IV.29

Chapter 1

PRANAYAMA, THE SHORTCUT TO IMMORTALITY

Pranayama, the ancient Science of Life challenges our preconceived notions of death and life and takes us on an incredible journey, where the impossible becomes possible.

Have you ever seen a dead body? Indeed, most of us have, even if it might only be a dead bird or a dead cat. Almost everyone considers all talk of death as macabre, but on closer look at the dead remains of a bee or some other insect, we discover that what was once an amazing lively creature is now nothing but dead matter. Life has left the body. *Prana* has left the body. This is what *prana* means: *prana* is life. The nature of *prana* is consciousness.

Meaning of Pranayama

Pranayama is a composite of two Sanskrit words: *prana* means "vitality," "the essence" or "the life force" and *ayama* means "mastery," "control" or "regulation." Pranayama is thus the mastery over the life force. Pranayama is also the mastery over the pauses in breath or over the transition between exhalation, inhalation and exhalation.

Difference between Breathing Exercises and Pranayama

Though important, breathing exercises are superficial. They are not considered to be pranayama; they prepare you for pranayama. Pranayama are deeper practices and can be done mentally. Through pranayama you can open the blocked energy channel known as sushumna and awaken the dormant energy in the body. This is not possible through mere breathing exercises. This may come as a surprise to those who are convinced that pranayama is only about breathing exercises. Many practitioners of physical culture, even many yoga teachers, believe that pranayama is nothing other than breathing exercises. Nothing can be further from the truth.

Difference between Breath and Prana

One of the most obvious aspects of prana is the breath, but the breath is not prana. Breath or air is known as *vayu*. An inflated balloon is also filled with air, but it is not living because it has no prana. Prana is something living, full of light and intelligence. If the breath were a horse, then prana would be the rider. It is prana that guides and directs the various functions of the body including respiration.

To understand the difference between breath and prana, we must first understand the yogic anatomy of a person. Most of us see ourselves just as a body. Some of us see ourselves as body as well as mind. Yogic literature provides a detailed analysis of who we are and what we are made up of (Fig. 1.1).

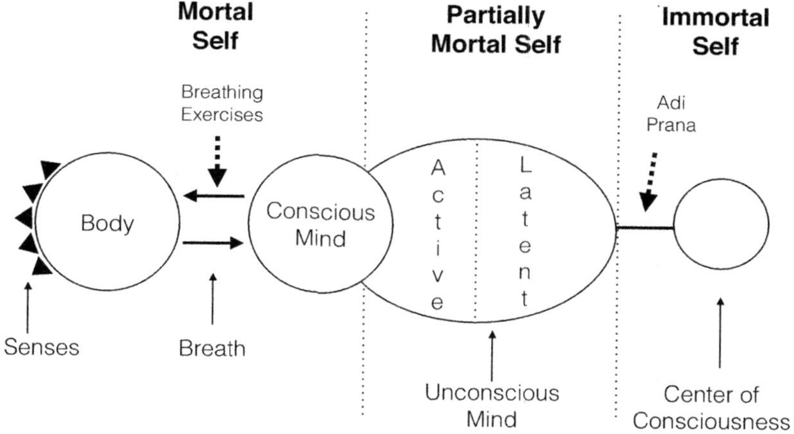

Figure 1.1 **Yogic Anatomy**

The yogic anatomy comprises of:

- the body
- the active and cognitive senses which interact with the external world
- the breath including exhalation and inhalation
- the conscious mind
- the active and latent unconscious mind
- *Adi* Prana, the first unit of energy
- and finally the Center of Consciousness

Adi means "the first." Prana, as we already know, is life. Thus Adi Prana is the first unit of life. Adi Prana is far subtler and finer than the breath and lies beyond the mind.

Breath and Mind

The breath is the bridge between the body and the senses on the grosser level, and the conscious and unconscious mind on the subtler level. The breath is a handle to the conscious and unconscious mind as well as the involuntary nervous system.

You have no control over the digestive system or the blood circulation in the body. These are regulated by the involuntary nervous system. You are breathing all the time; you do not have to remember to breathe. The breath is self regulated. If you need more oxygen, for instance, during exercise, the breath rate increases. The breath is controlled by the involuntary nervous system, yet at the same time you can also exercise control over it. This makes the breath unique. It can be used to gain control of the involuntary nervous system and the deeper aspects of the unconscious mind, since the breath gives us access to both, the voluntary as well as the involuntary nervous system.

> **Experiment**
>
> Observe your breath when you are relaxed and happy. How many seconds long is your exhalation and inhalation? Is your breath shallow or deep? Do you experience any jerks or pauses in the breath? Does the breath flow smoothly? Study your breath at different times of the day.

Observing the breath means observing the mind. If the mind is calm, the breath is calm. You can observe the correlation between your mental state and the breath. When you are angry, you breathe rapidly and the breath is very shallow. The primitive instinct of fight-or-flight manifests itself in the breath as the body prepares itself for a stressful situation. When you are shocked or scared, you tend to hold your breath. It is relatively difficult to observe the breath and study its nature when you are angry or afraid, since you are caught up in the situation. It is easier to study the breath when you are calm. You will observe that when you are relaxed, the breath is deep and slow. However, this is not a one-way relationship. The inverse is also true: calming your breath calms your mind.

Experiment

When you are disappointed or feeling lonely observe the breath. Is the breath short and shallow? Allow the breath to slow down and go deeper. Does the slow and deep breath help transform your mood?

You can use the breath as a handle to slowly gain mastery over the mind. However, mastery over the mind does not mean control and manipulation of the mind, it means witnessing the nature of the mind. Generally, you do not witness the thoughts in the mind, you just fall into whatever thought is rising up in the conscious mind. If it is a pleasant thought, you get attached to it and if it is an unpleasant thought, you experience aversion. Both attachment as well as aversion are twin sides of a single coin. By observing the breath you regain your awareness and are able to observe the mental states, which in turn helps calm the mind.

Guiding Principle

Observing the connection between breath and mind means learning to observe the mind.

Breath and Life Span

According to ancient yogic literature, when you come to this plane of existence your life span is predetermined. So you ask, how many years will I live? Years do not have any significance as a measure of life span; from a yogic perspective, the breath is a more reliable measure of life span.

Breath and life span have a mysterious relationship. According to yogic literature you come into the world with an allotted number of breaths. If you breathe fast, you use up the predetermined number of breaths faster. If you elongate your breath, breathing slowly, then you use up the predetermined number of breaths over a longer period of time. Thus, by breathing slowly, you stretch your life span.

To understand the relationship between breath and life span, observe the animal kingdom. Dogs are known to have a rapid breath. The breath rate of a dog at rest is between 10–30 breaths per minute, but they also pant at a rate of 200 breaths per minute. The higher the breath rate per minute, the shorter the life span. Not surprisingly, the life span of a dog is only around 8–12 years, few living over 12 years.

Elephants, on the other hand, breathe slower than dogs. When lying down, elephants have a breath rate of 4–5 breaths per minute and when standing, the breath rate increases to 10–12 breaths per minute. Wild Asian elephants live between 40–50 years and wild African elephants between 50–60 years. The giant tortoise, known for its long life span, breathes only 4–5 times per minute and has an average life span of 150 years. From these observations, the sages concluded that the breath rate has a clear influence on the life span.

TIP: Breathe slowly to live longer.

Those suffering from chronic stress in a competitive world are permanently functioning under the fight-or-flight mechanism. They have a shallow and rapid breath. The fight-or-flight response causes the muscles to stiffen up, the breathing apparatus goes into overdrive mode to pump in huge amounts of oxygen to fight or flee, and the posture changes. The constant fear and aggression causes the breathing pattern to be disturbed and does not return to its normal state. In fact, the fight-or-flight response has become the norm in our busy modern, urban lifestyle.

An important aspect of *Mastering Pranayama* is the remedial aspect of breathing exercises. It is not possible to progress without correction of wrong breathing patterns. Incorrect breathing patterns have to be unlearned. The re-establishment of slow, deep diaphragmatic breathing, together with the release of wastes and toxins, is an absolute necessity. It becomes clear that relaxation is not just at the muscular level; it is the release of toxins from the body as well as the mind.

Experiment

Visualize yourself running away from danger for a couple of minutes. You can imagine anything that you are really afraid of, such as an aggressive animal. How long do you think you can keep running away from this imaginary danger? How is your breathing? How is your mental state?

The kind of extreme stress most people leading an ambitious and competitive lifestyle are exposed to, is like being chased by an aggressive dog. From the visualization exercise it must be clear that chronic emotional stress, in this case the flight mode, can have a massive health impact. Obviously you cannot keep running for days or weeks. Yet, the modern person lives under this kind of stress for months, even years.

What happens when the breath slows down

Once a healthy breathing pattern has been re-established and the wastes and toxins have been released, the real work of mastering pranayama can start. Slowing down or elongating the breath allows you to observe your thoughts. Breath elongation is the key to understanding the conscious as well as the unconscious mind. It leads to the breathless state known as Kumbhaka and ultimately to Adi Prana, the nature of life itself. Adi Prana is also known as kundalini shakti.

Most teachers, claiming they can help you awaken the kundalini, teach you breathing exercises, but breathing exercises are superficial, remaining at the level of breath. Between the breath and Adi Prana lies the conscious mind and the deep and treacherous domain of the unconscious mind. You cannot reach the level of Adi Prana unless you have passed through the layers of the mind. Breathing exercises will help you to calm down your nervous system and prepare you for pranayama and the purification of the mind. Anyone can do breathing exercises but not everyone, it seems, can do pranayama.

Artists, writers, musicians and other creative people have unconsciously gained access to the potential of the unconscious mind. Though they have tapped only a small portion of the vast energy of the unconscious mind, this makes them bubble with creative energy. In other areas they still have to deal with their negative qualities that block the flow of this energy. The lack of a steady flow of energy causes a lot of suffering to creative persons. The yogic path, on the other hand, is a systematic path. It ensures that the practitioner proceeds step by step from grosser levels of the body and senses, past the breath and mind to the very source of all creative energy. This means beginning at the most external and gross level of the senses. Why do you get upset when somebody tells you, that your clothes look shabby? Why do you feel good when others admire your new car? Because you identify with these sensory objects. If you are strongly identified with the objects of the world, do not expect that you will suddenly experience prana itself. You need guidance and a systematic practice, which includes asanas, breathing exercises, learning meditation and purifying the conscious and unconscious mind over a long period of time. You must learn to look at your own negative qualities and to attenuate these. Few want to do this.

Benefits of Breathing Exercises

Breathing techniques such as Diaphragmatic Breathing and Equal Breathing are remedial in nature. The correction of wrong breathing releases great energy and gives you more self-confidence.

Many of the breathing practices are cleansing practices. Kapalabhati is one of the *shatkriyas* or six cleansing techniques. In Rechaka and Ujjayi a lot of carbon dioxide is removed from the lungs, and the blood is oxygenated. The removal of wastes is also extremely relaxing and invigorating. Bhastrika floods the body and brain with oxygen, and prepares it for the breathless state. This churns up a lot of energy. This energy is not comparable to tension or aggression; it has a different quality. Breathing exercises increase vitality, soothe the nervous system and calm the mind. All these practices lead to health at all levels.

Dangers of Incorrect Breathing Exercises

While breathing exercises are a preparation for pranayama practices and meditation, the manner in which these breathing exercises are generally practiced cannot lead to direct experience of prana. Untrained or poorly trained teachers organize what they call advanced pranayama seminars and workshops. They teach exercises like breath retention known as *Kumbhaka* and other complicated exercises. Many of these so-called teachers are just experimenting on their students while the students themselves remain unaware of the dangers of incorrectly practiced techniques, which can disturb the pranic vehicles.

Disturbance of pranic vehicles can lead to many imbalances causing, among others:

- Headaches
- Erratic mood changes

- Tendency to colds and congestion
- Dizziness
- Damage to finer lung tissue

Prolonged practice of incorrect breathing exercises can lead to permanent disturbance of the pranic vehicles.

For millennia, yogic literature was only available to the Oral Tradition and handed down from teacher to the student. This yogic literature was forbidden to those who were not part of that lineage. The student was prepared by the teacher and the practices were only given when the student was ready. Now that the yogic literature is freely available, it has become common practice to experiment with many techniques and the more complicated they are, the better. This has harmed students because incorrect breathing exercises and wrong pranayama practices disturb the pranic vehicles.

Most students and practitioners like to go to different teachers and different traditions over years and create their own "cut and paste" practice. Thus, many years are spent in experimentation and a lot of these practices are at best just useless and in the worse case counter-productive and harmful at a pranic level. All the faulty practices have to be unlearned. The unlearning process can take years and sometimes the damage cannot be undone. Therefore, breathing techniques and pranayama practices should be practiced under the guidance of highly experienced teachers of an unbroken lineage.

Precautionary Measures

Many people begin with complicated practices since they regard the simple practices as too easy. The complicated practices do not seem to benefit them and they do not really progress because they have skipped over the foundation. Fact is: simple practices take you deeper.

While the techniques and practices in *Mastering Pranayama* may seem harmless, caution is advised. These practices are best suited for healthy persons. Children and the aged should not be experimenting with these. Those with chronic health issues should consult a physician. Menstruating and pregnant women are advised not to practice these techniques without guidance. When in doubt seek out a well trained and experienced teacher.

Rather than doing a lot of different techniques, it is advisable to focus on a couple of simple remedial exercises to start with. Follow these two simple guidelines:

- Avoid teachers that mix practices from different traditions.
- If you do not find a qualified and experienced teacher, then practice and master diaphragmatic breathing.

Mastering Pranayama is divided into two major sections. In the foundational part the most important breathing exercises are covered. This section lays great emphasis on correcting the poor breathing patterns of the average modern person and preparing the student for the next level. Correct breathing exercises lead to pranayama if done systematically and integrated gradually in your life. In the advanced section, hopefully the difference between breathing exercises and pranayama will become clear through direct experience.

Chapter 2

ARE YOU BREATHING RIGHT?

No one ever asked you this question before and you never thought about it. Unfortunately it is true: most of us do not know how to breathe right. Lesson one is unlearning wrong breathing habits.

Have you ever tried to hold your breath?

Most children experiment with the breath underwater while swimming and discover that they can hold their breath only for 5–10 seconds without any prior training. After years of intense training a free diver can hold his breath for several minutes, although at grave risk to his health and life. If you have not had any prior training then within seconds your lungs seem to be bursting and every cell in your body seems to be crying for air. Breath is so vital to life, one would imagine that we would be a little more aware of this vital function, but we are not. Most people following a hectic urban lifestyle breathe incorrectly.

Experiment

Do not do any special breathing practices before you test your breath retention capacity. Hold your breath and time it. No cheating!

Why is our breathing incorrect?

It is fascinating to watch newborns breathe. Babies breathe naturally and instinctively; they breathe deep and use their diaphragm. But by the age of 5–6 years many children have shallow chest breathing. Apart from the development of the chest area, there are three reasons for this:

1. Tight clothes: Everyone wants to look good and keep up with the fashions of the time. This means that even little children wear tight clothes such as leggings and trousers that sit on the abdomen and create an obstacle to the movement of the diaphragm. These tight clothes are uncomfortable for the children, but since they cannot express themselves, they have no choice but to wear them. The body is forced into chest breathing, which eventually becomes a deep-rooted habit.

2. Competitive and hectic lifestyle: The constant pressure to perform keeps the body in the fight-or-flight response mode. In the previous chapter you visualized the flight response. In the following exercise you will visualize the fight response.

Experiment

Imagine you are being attacked by a vicious dog. You are cornered and you cannot run away. You have no choice but to fight. Take your time to visualize this in detail. How is your breathing? How is your mental state? Most important, how is your posture?

With a little imagination it would be clear that in a dangerous situation, like being cornered by a vicious dog, the posture is no longer relaxed. The muscles stiffen up and shoulders are lifted in a defensive posture. The breathing is shallow, rapid and agitated. Fear and anxiety are the predominant mental states. This is exactly how a person behaves when experiencing pressure and competition. If the pressure and competition is constant, the defensive posture becomes a habit. Then eventually shallow and rapid breathing also becomes normal for such a person.

Correcting the posture is difficult because whenever such a person tries to relax his shoulders and let down his guard he feels vulnerable and defenseless, creating a state of anxiety, which strengthens the vicious circle. Instead, one can correct the faulty breathing pattern, which would lead to an improvement in the mental state of anxiety and eventually allow the person to relax physically as well as mentally. The practitioner must unlearn the old breathing habits and relearn new breathing and postural habits.

3. Self Image: The third reason is an interesting phenomenon that seems to have taken over the modern world. Modern society promotes the image of a broad chest and a narrow waist as the ideal of health and beauty. To breath diaphragmatically would disturb this image.

How to correct faulty breathing

There are a number of things you can do to change this for yourself as well as for others:

- Do not make infants and children wear tight clothes.
- Baby diapers should not be too tight. Leave two-finger space for the baby or infant to breathe freely.
- Wear loose fitting and comfortable clothing at least at home.
- Do not reinforce this contrived self-image of health and beauty.
- Learn to breathe correctly.

The 7 Step Program

Now that you have understood why most of us breathe incorrectly, we come to the core of *Mastering Pranayama*: the 7 Step Program. This program takes you step by step from simple remedial techniques to advanced practices. At first, the program may seem too simple, but on deeper study and practice, you will discover it to be challenging. Remember, the best of practitioners fail because they are overconfident and skip the basics. Do not overestimate your own capacity. Begin slowly and expand your capacity gradually.

The 7 Step Program includes:

1. establishing natural and effortless diaphragmatic breathing
2. establishing the even or equal breath, that is, the length of exhalation is equal to the length of inhalation
3. establishing silent breathing
4. establishing smooth breathing, that is, no jerky breathing
5. eliminating pauses between exhalation, inhalation and exhalation
6. establishing the elongated breath, that is, increasing the length of exhalation and inhalation
7. beginning to understand, experience and eventually attain mastery over prana itself

The best of practitioners would require at least eight months until Step 6 is mastered. The average practitioner, who does not practice every day, would require at least a year to integrate this method into his life. It is important that you neither rush through the program nor push your body beyond its limits.

Step 1 retrains the muscles and re-establishes correct breathing habit patterns that are natural and effortless. This is important for everyone, irrespective of whether you aspire to practice advanced pranayama or not. It is the basis of good health. Steps 2–6 refine the breath, remove wastes and energize the mind and body; these increase well-being and energy. The actual practice of pranayama begins only at Step 7.

Criteria for a Natural and Optimal Respiratory Pattern

Babies breathe naturally and spontaneously. No one teaches them how to breathe. Observe a baby breathing and you will see the abdomen lifting and falling. This is diaphragmatic breathing. This is the correct way of breathing. The slow and regular movement clearly indicates that the breathing is deep and even.

An absolute basic requirement for natural optimal breathing is using the muscle called the diaphragm while breathing. Diaphragmatic Breathing is the single most important practice to learn before beginning any other breathing exercises. To understand and correctly practice diaphragmatic breathing you must know that the human body is made up of head, torso and the four limbs.

The torso can be divided into the following:

- the thorax or chest, which houses the two lungs
- the diaphragm, a tough sheet of muscle, which separates the chest from the digestive organs in the abdominal region
- the pelvis, which extends from the hip bones to the organs of excretion and reproduction

One can fill the lungs in three ways:

- extending the diaphragm downward, called diaphragmatic breathing
- expanding the walls of the chest outward, called thoracic or chest breathing
- moving the shoulder area called clavicular breathing

If your breath is rapid and shallow you are probably chest breathing. This means you are using only part of the lungs' capacity. Diaphragmatic breathing is physiologically the most efficient from the three types of breathing. The goal is to re-establish the body's natural respiratory pattern called even, diaphragmatic breathing.

How Diaphragmatic Breathing works

In the resting position the diaphragm billows up into the chest cavity like a dome. For this reason its movements are not directly visible at the body's surface.

Diaphragmatic inhalation is accomplished by moving the diaphragm downward. As the diaphragm moves downward, it decreases the volume of the abdominal cavity, so that the abdomen moves outward and the lungs expand (Fig. 2.1a). The lungs are very elastic and expansive; when they are efficiently filled, their capacity is far greater than with shallow chest breathing.

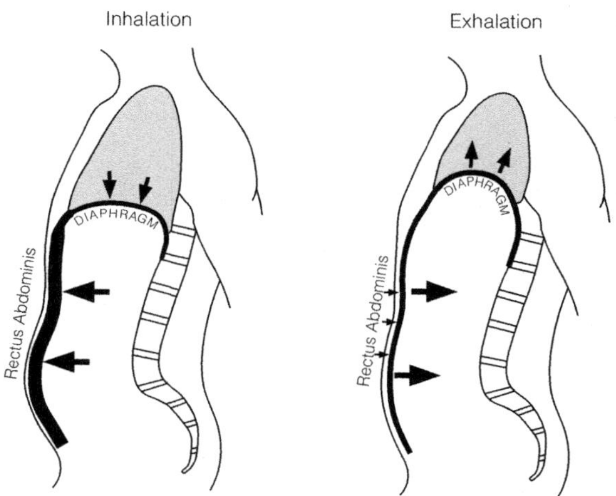

Figure 2.1a **Diaphragmatic & Abdominal Muscles**

As the diaphragm moves up, the lungs are emptied; as the diaphragm comes down the lungs are filled (Fig. 2.1b). You cannot really observe the diaphragm muscle but when you breath diaphragmatically you may notice that the lower ribs and the abdominal area flare out slightly. On exhalation the abdominal area moves back inward.

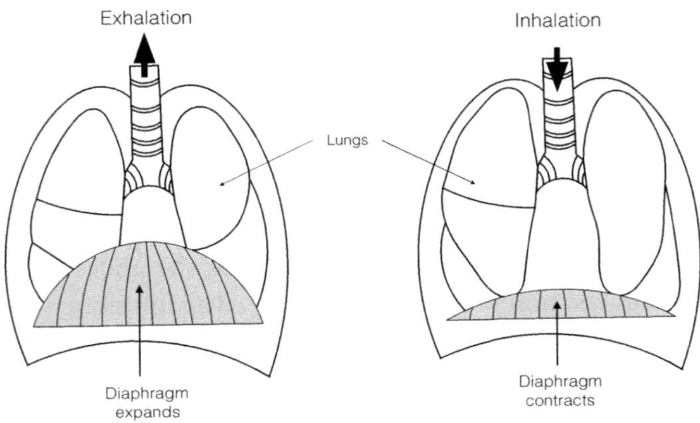

Figure 2.1b **Diaphragmatic Breathing**

Are you breathing right?

Diaphragmatic Breathing is not a pranayama practice. It is a breathing exercise meant to re-establish the natural breathing pattern. If you have unlearned your natural and healthy breathing pattern, like the most of us have, then you need to re-establish it. You must retrain yourself to use the diaphragm over a period of time and re-establish this as your normal breathing pattern. You should plan to spend four weeks consciously learning how to breathe diaphragmatically before you turn your attention to the other breathing exercises and pranayama.

Experiment

You can check your breath in a normal seated position by placing one hand on the chest and the other on the abdomen (Fig. 2.2). If you are breathing diaphragmatically, the hand on the abdomen will rise and fall, while the hand on the chest will not.

There is only one practice, which is safe without guidance of any sort and that is Diaphragmatic Breathing. Anybody and everybody can do Diaphragmatic Breathing. There are simple techniques that strengthen the diaphragm and retrain the breathing pattern. You can do these techniques even if you do not have access to a qualified and experienced teacher.

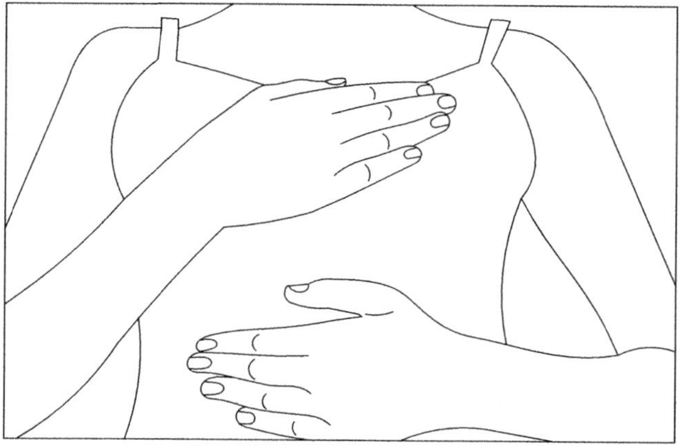

Figure 2.2 **Hands on Chest and Abdomen**

Diaphragmatic Breathing and Posture

It is difficult to breathe diaphragmatically unless the head, the neck and the trunk of the body are correctly aligned. Therefore, the posture is important while practicing diaphragmatic breathing. If your posture is poor you will not be able to breathe freely because you will unconsciously constrict the movement of the diaphragm.

Experiment

Sit upright on the edge of a straight backed chair with both your feet firmly placed on the floor. Observe your breath. Notice how your abdomen can freely expand. Now slouch down in the same position, so that your spine is curved, your chest cramped and your arms fall to the sides of your legs. Notice how difficult it is to breathe in this position. This dramatic difference in position shows the importance of a good posture.

There are interesting interactions between the diaphragm and gravity, depending on the posture. If the body is in an upright posture, gravity tends to pull downward on the abdominal contents, the diaphragm and the lungs facilitating inhalation. When one lies flat on the back, the diaphragm pushes the abdominal wall upward during inhalation. Little or no muscular effort is needed for diaphragmatic exhalation in this position. This makes the horizontal body position interesting for training diaphragmatic breathing and re-establishing even breath.

How to train Diaphragmatic Breathing

There are two useful techniques to train the diaphragm muscle and help you become aware of diaphragmatic breathing. Before you start practicing these two techniques, you should be able to locate the diaphragm.

Locating your diaphragm

Place both hands on the sides of your chest. You can easily feel the ribs. Feel the lowest ribs on the sides with your thumb, while the remaining fingers feel the area in front of the body. This is where the diaphragm is located within the rib cage. It divides the torso in two parts: the chest and the abdomen.

Shavasana

Shavasana is also known as the Corpse Pose. Lie on your back on a mat on the floor with a thin pillow or shawl under the head. Keep the arms away from the body and the feet slightly apart (Fig. 2.3a).

As you inhale the abdomen rises; as you exhale the abdomen falls (Fig. 2.3b).

If you are breathing diaphragmatically you will feel little or no movement of the upper chest. During this practice allow the mind's eye to focus on the abdominal area since it is difficult to locate the diaphragm itself. This is a good posture to retrain the diaphragmatic muscles because it requires no guidance and it is almost effortless. It can be practiced as often as you want, any time of the day.

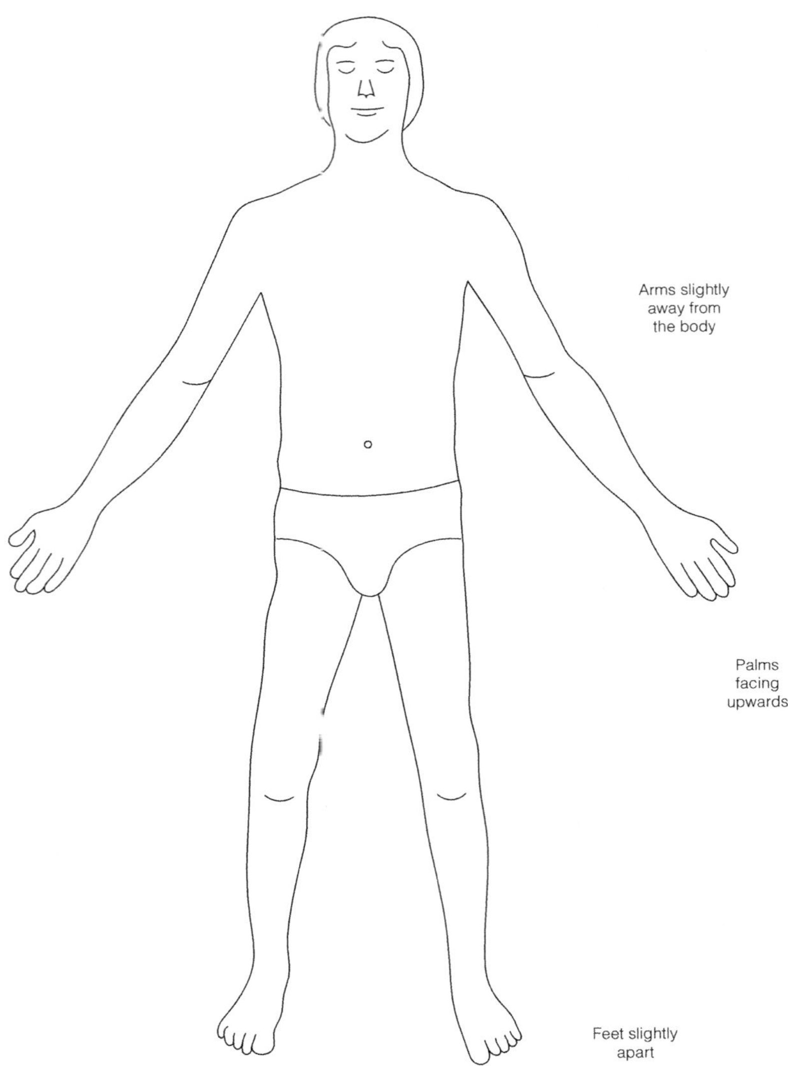

Figure 2.3a **Shavasana**

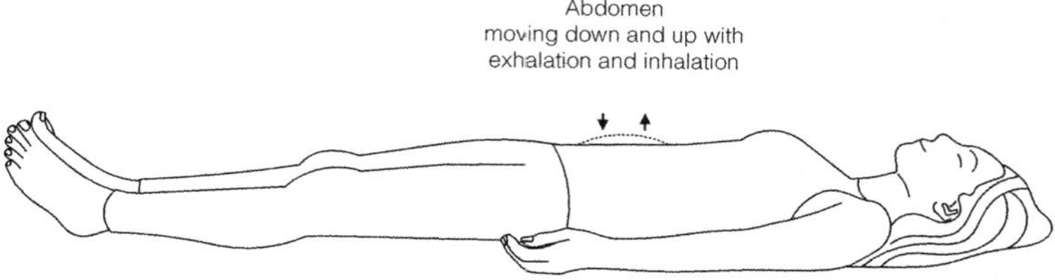

Figure 2.3b **Shavasana**

You may also fold the legs together in this position if you want to train diaphragmatic breathing for a longer period of time. This will support the lower back. You may place one hand on the abdomen and feel it rise and fall (Fig. 2.4).

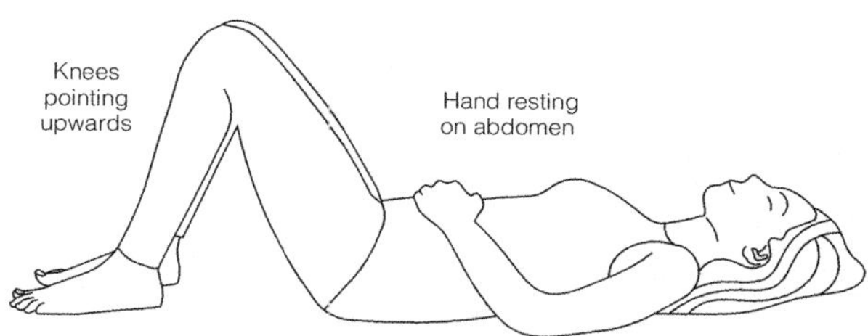

Figure 2.4 **Diaphragmatic Breathing with Folded Legs**

Makarasana

Makarasana is also known as the Crocodile Pose. Lie on the stomach, placing the feet a comfortable distance apart from each other and pointing the toes outward. Fold the arms in front of the body, resting the hands on the lower arms. Position the arms so that the chest does not touch the floor. Let the head rest on the arms (Fig. 2.5). This posture necessitates diaphragmatic breathing. When you inhale you feel the abdomen pressed against the floor and when you exhale you feel the abdominal muscles relaxing. Breathing for around five minutes, twice a day, morning and evening in this position can help make diaphragmatic breathing a natural habit.

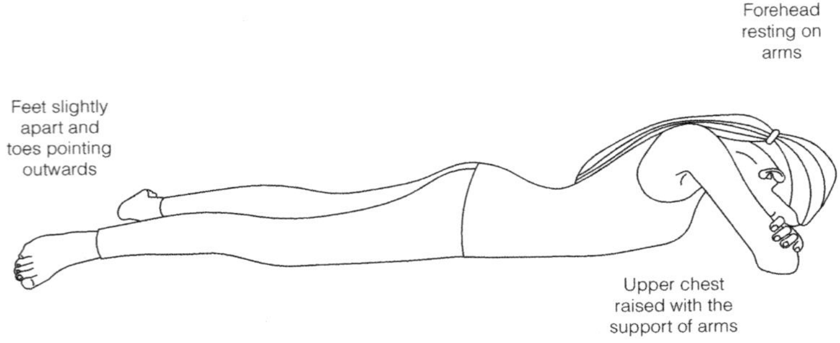

Figure 2.5 **Makarasana Variation 2**

Diaphragmatic breathing in Makarasana Variation 2 is like weight lifting. This posture is superior to Shavasana to retrain the diaphragm since the muscle has to work hard to lift the weight of the entire torso. Unfortunately it is not possible to stay in this posture for long because the "weight lifting" is strenuous and also because the shoulders and upper arms start hurting in this position after a while. Makarasana Variation 1 is relaxing, but it is not suitable to retrain the diaphragm. Makarasana Variation 1 (Fig. 2.6) can be used to rest should Makarasana Variation 2 get too strenuous. You can use the two variations alternately if you train for longer periods of time.

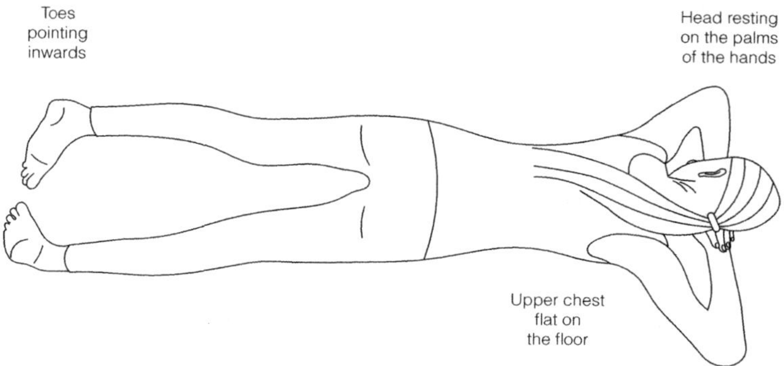

Figure 2.6 **Makarasana Variation 1**

Intensive retraining of the diaphragm with the help of Shavasana and Makarasana over four weeks will help you re-establish healthy breathing patterns. Makarasana is not suitable for pregnant women.

Equal Diaphragmatic Breathing

Once the diaphragm has been retrained, you can focus on the finer criteria for natural respiration. A clear sign that you need to work on the finer aspects of the breath is when you speak too fast or you are holding your breath unconsciously and then gasping to catch your breath.

In equal, diaphragmatic breathing all exhalations and inhalations are more or less equal in length. The breath flows through the nostrils and not through the mouth. To establish equal, diaphragmatic breathing you allow the lungs to expand fully with the inhalation and to be emptied with the exhalation, so that the volume of air inhaled is equal to the volume of air exhaled.

You can train Equal Breathing in Shavasana. Focus the mind on the diaphragm or abdominal area. With the mind's eye watch the abdomen rise and fall. Fill your lungs with air slowly and allow the air to be exhaled slowly. When the breathing slows down, the breath finds its natural balance and equalizes.

Smooth out Irregularities of the Breath

On regular practice of equal, diaphragmatic breathing in Shavasana, you will observe four irregularities of the breath.

Jerky breath: This may be caused by rapid speech, stress or wrong breathing habits. These can be unlearned by observation and conscious effort to breathe smoothly during equal diaphragmatic breathing.

Noisy breath: As you listen carefully to the breath, you will notice that when exhalation and inhalation is absolutely silent then the breath becomes fine and subtle. To an external observer it may even appear that you are no longer breathing.

Pauses between exhalation, inhalation and exhalation: As the breath gets finer and subtler you will find yourself being disturbed by involuntary pauses between exhalation and inhalation and between inhalation and exhalation. Focus on eliminating these pauses.

Shallow breath: As your breath becomes finer and the involuntary pauses are eliminated, you will find to your surprise that the duration of each breath naturally increases. With conscious effort you can further elongate the breath.

While these four irregularities are to be observed and smoothed out during the practice of Diaphragmatic Breathing, you will revisit these in the ongoing process of mastering pranayama.

Limitations

With regular practice of equal, diaphragmatic breathing you will begin to observe some obstacles that disturb your practice, such as:

Mild Cold and Cough

If your nose is blocked, you cannot do many breathing practices, especially those that help establish a finer and subtle breath without pauses. It is best to wait until you are healthy again.

Acute Infections

When you have acute infections of any kind you should not do heavy breathing exercises. Reduce breathing exercises to gentle Diaphragmatic Breathing during acute problems.

Chronic Conditions

If you have a chronic respiratory problem, it is best to seek guidance. Those with severe asthma, bronchitis or other respiratory disorders should practice breathing exercises under the guidance of an experienced teacher. The only breathing exercise that is safe to do at all times is Diaphragmatic Breathing.

Jalaneti: A Cleansing Technique

Jalaneti is a very useful cleansing practice which is done best in conjunction with a healthy, balanced diet. It removes excess mucus from the mucus membranes in the nostrils and throat with the aid of a salt water bath. This practice can be done with or without the neti pot.

Avoid practicing Jalaneti when you have a cold, a cough or a sore throat. Never practice Jalaneti if you are suffering from an acute infection. Jalaneti can aggravate acute infections. Jalaneti is a cleansing practice that is preventive in nature. Also do not practice Jalaneti before bedtime. If you have not freed the nostrils completely of salt water, this can flow into the sinuses as you lay down in the horizontal position and cause aggravations.

Preparation of Jalaneti Water

The water used for Jalaneti should be clean and free of microbes. For this purpose it is best to use lukewarm drinking water. Hot as well as cold water cause discomfort. Gradually add salt to the lukewarm water until the water has the same consistency of salt as your tears. Too much salt will cause a burning and stinging experience; too little salt prevents the water from flowing freely and easily through the nostrils. When the salt water tastes right, it is ready for Jalaneti.

With Neti Pot

Take a neti pot and rinse it out with clean drinking water. Fill the pot with the lukewarm salt water you have prepared. Tilt your head to the left and bend slightly forward. Press the snout of the neti pot into your right nostril and pour in a little salt water. It should flow out of the left nostril easily. Put down the pot and stand erect with your head straight. Using your right index finger, close your right nostril and blow rapidly 3–4 times out of the left nostril. This should release some mucus stuck in the left nostril.

Now, tilt your head to the right and bend slightly forward. Press the snout of the neti pot into your left nostril and pour in a little salt water. It should flow out of the right nostril easily (Fig. 2.7). Stand erect with your head straight. Using your left index finger, close your left nostril and blow rapidly 3–4 times out of the right nostril. This should release some mucus stuck in the right nostril.

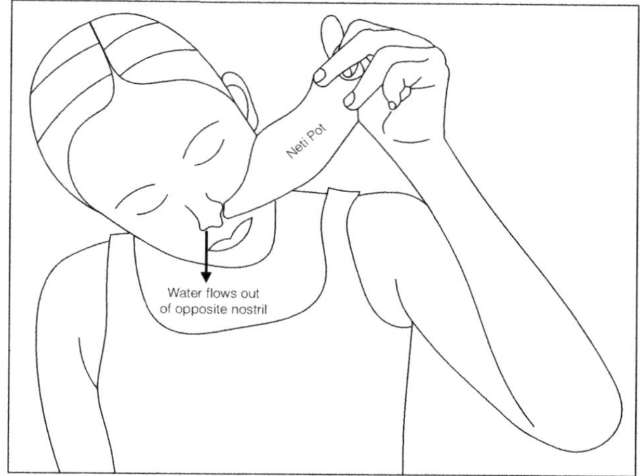

Figure 2.7 **Jalaneti with Neti Pot**

Practice Jalaneti regularly by integrating it into your morning ritual of cleaning your face and teeth. After this you can practice different breathing practices comfortably since both nostrils are free.

This method is passive in comparison to the active method of practicing Jalaneti without a neti pot.

Without Neti Pot

Jalaneti can also be done without a neti pot. Keep the lukewarm salt water in a glass instead of a neti pot.

Cup the palm of your right hand, while you hold the glass in the left hand. Pour a little salt water into the right hand and immediately put down the glass. Now bend your head forward, close the left nostril with the left index finger and "inhale" the water through the right nostril (Fig. 2.8).

Figure 2.8 **Jalaneti with Hands**

The lukewarm salt water will flow into the mouth cavity. You can easily spit it out. Using your left index finger, close your left nostril again and blow rapidly 3–4 times out of the right nostril. This should release some mucus stuck in the right nostril.

Now cup the palm of your left hand, while you hold the glass in the right hand. Pour a little salt water into the left hand and immediately put down the glass. Bend your head forward, close the right nostril with the right index finger and "inhale" the water through the left nostril. The lukewarm salt water will flow into the mouth cavity. You can easily spit it out. Using your right index finger, close your right nostril again and blow rapidly 3–4 times out of the left nostril. This should release some mucus stuck in the left nostril.

The first experience of Jalaneti without a neti pot may be uncomfortable, since the experience of inhaling water is similar to drowning. However, it is superior to the passive version of using a neti pot. This method makes you independent of the neti pot and you can practice Jalaneti anywhere as long as you have clean, warm drinking water, some salt and a glass. If you are practicing Jalaneti for the first time it might be better to start with the passive method of using the neti pot and gradually move on to the method without the neti pot.

Q&A

Question: I always thought that the best way of breathing was using all three kinds of breathing, that is, diaphragmatic, thoracic and clavicular, in order to use full lung capacity. Please comment.

Answer: Using all three kinds of breathing, that is, diaphragmatic, thoracic and clavicular breathing, is necessary only when the body requires access to huge amounts of air for respiration, for instance, when performing sports. To breathe like this normally would put the body under a great deal of strain. In fact, you would put the body into the fight-or-flight response even though it is not necessary. This would have a serious impact on your health in the long term.

The most gentle and natural form of breathing is diaphragmatic breathing and it is very easy to train.

Chapter 3

FINDING THE BEST POSTURE OR THE SCIENCE OF SITTING

With seven postures to choose from, sitting is not just sitting. Lesson two is finding the right posture and preparing a comfortable seat. It may not look like it, but this is one of the most challenging stages of the journey. Don't give up before you have really started.

Once you have corrected faulty respiratory patterns and smoothed some of the irregularities in your breath, you are ready to start other breathing exercises. Most of these breathing exercises are best done in the seated position. Sitting on a chair is a good start, but it is important to graduate to a seated, meditative posture. In this chapter we will examine the different seated postures and find the best posture for you.

Postures for Pranayama: Seated and Supine

There are different breathing exercises and pranayama practices: some can be done in the seated position and others while lying flat on the back. For beginners or for those who are not able to do advanced pranayama, the seated posture is recommended, since most practitioners tend to fall asleep while lying down for a longer session of pranayama.

Breathing exercises such as Equal Breathing and Rechaka can be done in both, seated and supine positions. Other breathing exercises like Bhastrika, Kapalabhati, Ujjayi, Bhramari are best done in the seated position.

The seated postures are:

- Maitri Asana, the Friendship Pose
- Sukhasana, the Easy Pose
- Vajrasana, the Thunderbolt Pose
- Ardha Padmasana, the Half Lotus Pose
- Padmasana, the Lotus Pose
- Svastikasana, the Auspicious Pose
- Siddhasana, the Accomplished Pose

Five Important Criteria for a Seated Posture

There are five important criteria for the ideal seated posture (Fig. 3.1).

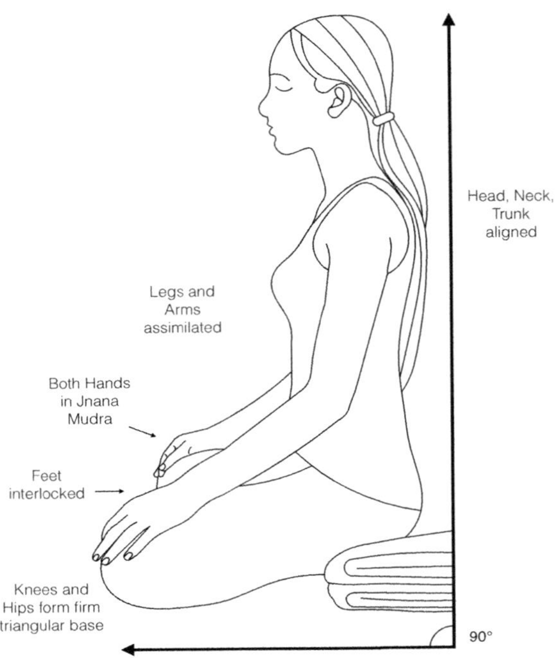

Figure 3.1 **Important Criteria for Seated Posture – Svastikasana**

1. Head-Neck-Trunk aligned: The most important criteria for a meditative pose is that the head, neck and trunk are aligned. The ancient Yoga handbook, the *Bhagavad Gita (VI.13)* says: *Samam kayashirahgrivam,* that is, "keeping your trunk, head and neck aligned." *Kaya* means "body," *shirah* means "head" and *grivam* means "neck." The head, neck and trunk should be straight and perpendicular to the ground or floor. This is very important, irrespective of the posture you sit in. This criterion needs to be observed in all the seated postures.
2. Firm Triangular Base: When the knees and hips form a firm base that is triangular in shape, the body weight is well distributed, and the knees and ankles do not hurt. The stable base also ensures that the upper torso does not sway.

3. Legs and Arms assimilated: In the seated posture one tries to keep the extremities as close to the body as possible.
4. Feet interlocked: Interlocking the legs and feet together ensures compactness of the body and prevents you from jumping up and out of meditation.
5. Jnana Mudra: *Jnana* means "knowledge." *Mudra* means both "a seal" or "closing." Jnana Mudra is the seal of knowledge. Mudras have a subtle but powerful influence on our minds; you will learn more about the mudras in Chapter 12. In Jnana Mudra the thumb and index finger touch each other in what is known as the pincer grip position (Fig. 3.2). The pincer grip indicates fine motor abilities that are a major factor in human development. When you sit applying Jnana Mudra, the palms should rest on the knees with fingers pointing downward. If you keep your palms open and your fingers pointing upward, they will always be against gravity. When you keep them pointing downward, they are completely relaxed. This is possible in all seated postures.

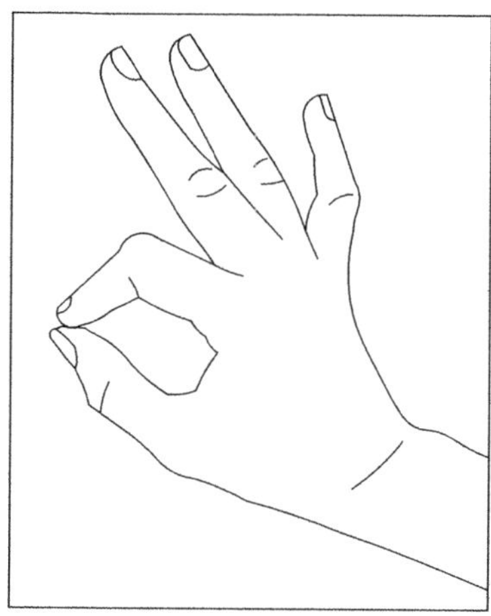

Figure 3.2 **Jnana Mudra**

Maitri Asana: The Friendship Pose

Maitri Asana or the Friendship Pose is a good pose for those, who are not flexible enough to sit on the floor, for those who are overweight, for those with arthritic problems or for those having physical problems such as injuries, which prevent them from sitting in a cross-legged position on the floor.

Sit comfortably on a straight backed chair. Sit, so that the feet rest flat on the ground (Fig. 3.3). Keep a mat, carpet or shawl under the feet to prevent them from getting cold. The mat should insulate against the cold floor. Cotton does not insulate well, so a thick woolen carpet or a silk shawl would be appropriate.

While Maitri Asana is easy and comfortable, the legs hang down on the floor. They are away from the torso and are not assimilated. Besides this, sitting in Maitri Asana means that you will not train for the meditative posture.

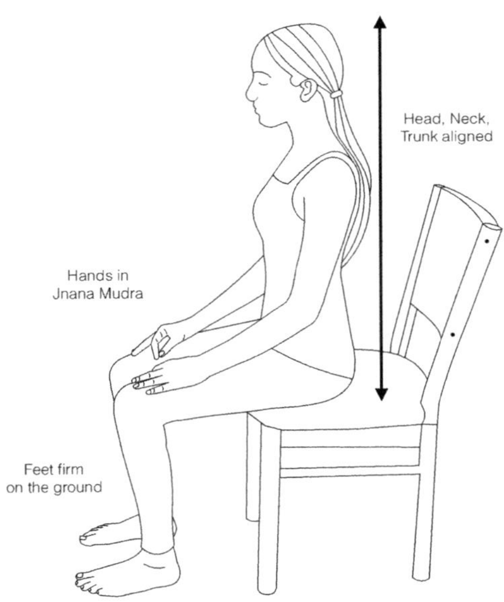

Figure 3.3 **Maitri Asana**

How to make a Meditation Seat

The seated meditative postures are always practiced on the floor or on the ground. However, it is not advisable to sit directly on the bare floor or ground without insulation. For a good meditation seat, you need to have a mat so that you do not feel cold on the bare floor or ground.

The *Bhagavad Gita* describes a meditation seat made out of cloth, deer skin and kusha grass. This recommendation comes from a time when the only persons who practiced meditation were wandering sages and hermits, who sat for meditation on the jungle floor or in the dirt of a mountain. Animal skin was ideal under the circumstances since it was easy to keep clean, the tough skin was not damaged by sharp stones or thorns in the jungle and it provided perfect insulation even in the coldest winter.

Having to sit on the hard, uneven and cold ground must have been uncomfortable, therefore these wandering sages developed a seat that was well insulated with grass and deer skin, one on top of the other. The first layer of kusha grass provided comfort and stability on the hard and uneven ground. The second layer of animal skin provided insulation against the cold floor that would otherwise upset the energy balance in the body. A cloth was used as a prop or to stabilize the seat. This detailed description indicates the importance of having a good seat.

In the early stages of practice it is not necessary to use animal skin. In advanced stages of meditation the practitioner may become sensitive to very slight changes in the energy and may prefer to use an animal skin seat instead of a woolen blanket or silk shawls. You do not need to buy meditation mats that are commercially available. These are generally made of synthetic fabrics which do not breathe. For a modern practitioner, soft woolen blankets and silk shawls will suffice. Use natural fabrics, as far as possible. You can sit in meditation in the comfort of your home on a seat that is well insulated, such as a woolen blanket. Cover the woolen blanket with a silk shawl so that the woolen blanket does not itch the skin. If you would like to enjoy the comfort of animal skin, you will find that the insulation of an animal skin such as sheepskin, which is commonly available in many countries, is excellent.

Vajrasana: The Thunderbolt Pose

Vajra means "thunderbolt."

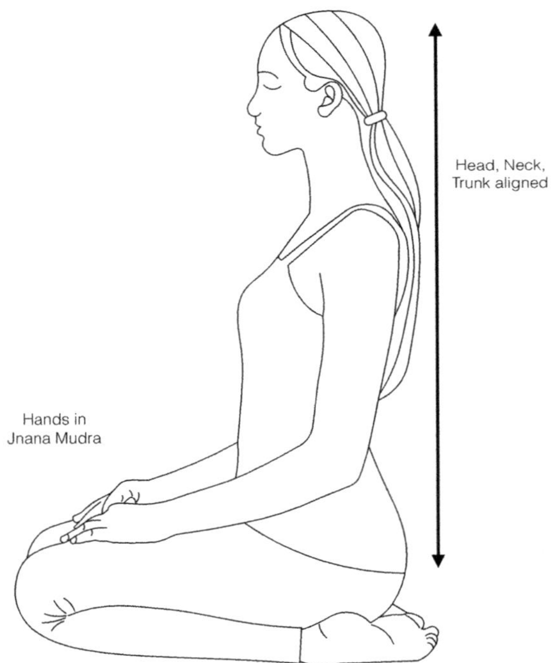

Figure 3.4 **Vajrasana**

Sit on the meditation seat with legs folded and the buttocks resting on the ankles. In the first variation of the Thunderbolt, the weight of the body lies heavily on the ankles. You cannot sit in this pose for longer than a few minutes. To master the posture you need flexibility of the lower limbs, until the weight of the body rests between the legs and the feet point inward (Fig. 3.4). It is still not a suitable posture to sit in for a longer period of time.

The main reason that Vajrasana is not used for pranayama practice is because it does not provide a firm base. Without a firm base, the upper torso is not steady and stable. Postures that provide a firm and steady triangular base are to be preferred.

Sukhasana: The Easy Pose

Sukha means "content" or "happy."

In Sukhasana, head, neck and trunk are aligned, the hands are placed on the knees in Jnana Mudra and the legs are crossed. In Sukhasana each foot is placed on the floor under the opposite knee (Fig. 3.5a). If you have never sat cross legged before, then Sukhasana is a good posture to start with.

A lot of people who sit cross legged on the floor experience discomfort because the back is often not completely aligned. There is a strong tendency to slouch after a while; this causes a pain in the neck and lower back (Fig. 3.5b). The knees and hips do not form a firm base for the body to rest on, since the knees point upward. The weight of the body is unevenly distributed causing discomfort to the ankles. The posture is not stable since the body weight rests only on the buttocks. As you relax in this posture, the knees seem to get heavier due to the pull of gravity (Fig. 3.5a).

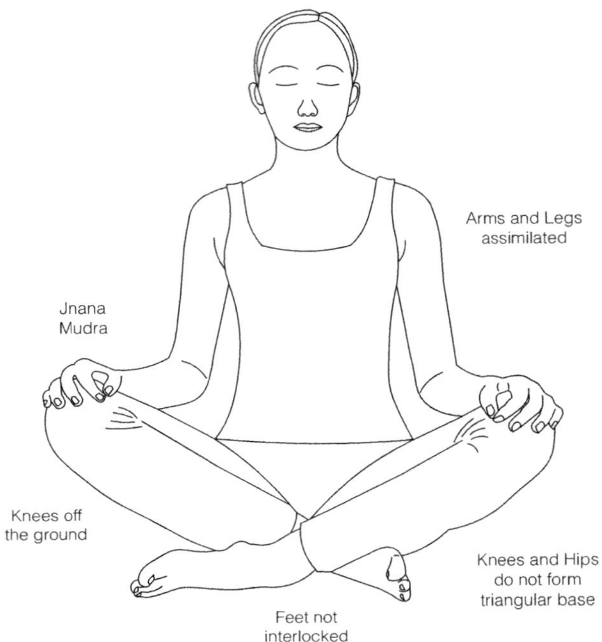

Figure 3.5a **Sukhasana – Frontal View**

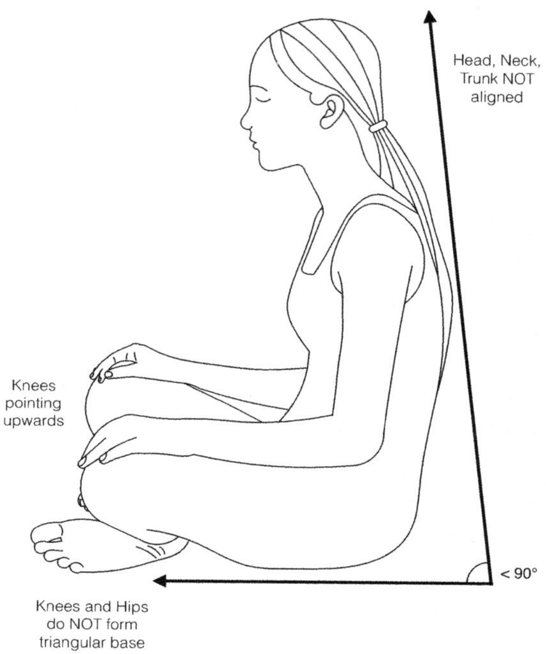

Figure 3.5b **Sukhasana – WRONG Technique**

Sukhasana has an advantage over Maitri Asana, that is the legs are assimilated, but all the same you are not able to sit very comfortably with your head, neck and trunk perpendicular to the floor. You can sit on a cushion, but it is better to use layers of thin cotton or silk shawls. The advantage of thin shawls over thick blankets is that you can make a seat of thin layers. With time, as you will sit longer in this pose, you can remove one shawl after the other, until you have mastered the position; the shawls are only a temporary prop. Keep the shawls long and flat in a rectangular shape. Do not fold them into squares, this makes the seat bulky and uncomfortable. You do not need to purchase any expensive contraptions for sitting such as crescent cushions, stools or benches.

This is what you need to make a comfortable seat; experiment with these until you have mastered the posture:

- 1 thick woolen blanket (or sheepskin) for the base
- 1 silk shawl to cover the base blanket
- 6–7 thin cotton shawls for layers
- 4–5 additional cotton shawls to support knees (only if required)
- 1 thick woolen blanket or thick shawl to cover the body

You can now sit on the meditation seat you have made with layers of thin cotton shawls so that you do not slouch. The pose is more comfortable with layers of shawls but the knees are still not firm on the ground (Fig. 3.5c). The feet are pointing outward and are not entirely assimilated in this posture. There is also an unconscious tendency to come out of the cross legged position and stretch out the legs.

You can sit in Sukhasana for a while and when you find yourself tiring or the back starts hurting then move to the chair and continue doing your practices on the chair in Maitri Asana. This is recommended only if you are unable to sit comfortably in the cross-legged position over a longer period of time.

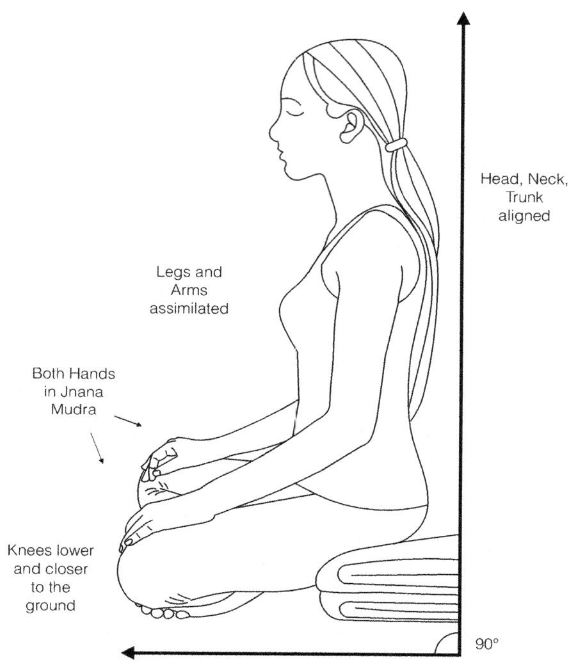

Figure 3.5c **Sukhasana with Layers**

Ardha Padmasana: The Half Lotus Pose

Ardha means "half." *Padma* means "lotus."

Sit on your meditation blanket. Bend your right leg and place the right foot on the left thigh. Alternatively, you can bend your left leg and place the left foot on the right thigh. Keep the fingers in Jnana Mudra. This is the Half Lotus Pose (Fig. 3.6).

Ardha Padmasana provides a firm base since both the knees are on the floor. You can also assimilate the legs well but only one of the feet is locked. It is a good exercise for the ankles and not as difficult as Padmasana. You can also use layers of thin shawls to master this pose gradually.

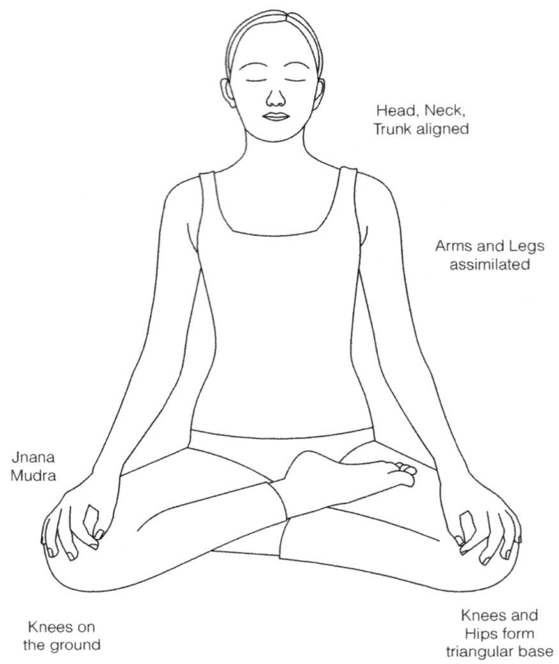

Figure 3.6 **Ardhapadmasana**

Padmasana: The Lotus Pose

Padmasana is the symbol of Yoga. Yogis, sages and saints are often seen sitting in Padmasana in ancient sculptures or paintings.

Sit on your meditation blanket. Bend your right leg and place the right foot on the left thigh, then bend your left leg and place the left foot on the right thigh; vice versa is also possible. This is the Lotus Pose (Fig. 3.7).

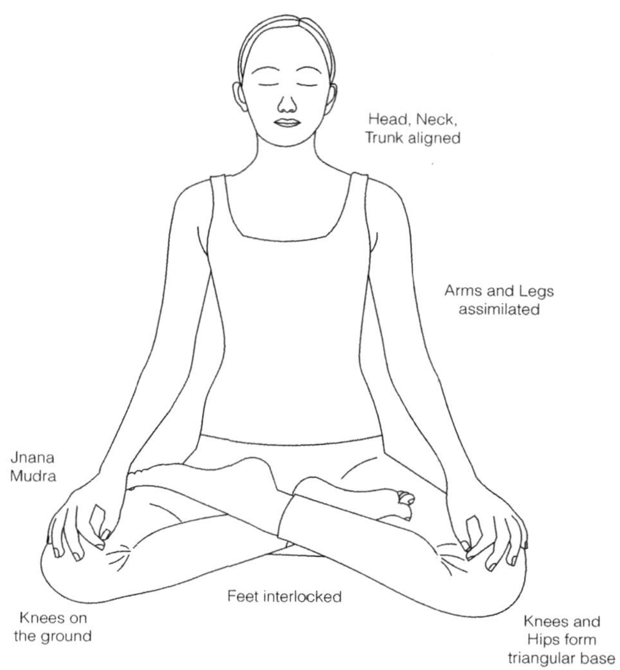

Figure 3.7 **Padmasana**

In Padmasana both the legs are well assimilated and the feet are completely interlocked. It is neither possible to unconsciously come out of this position nor to slip out of it. It is best to master the Half Lotus Pose before you attempt the Lotus Pose.

Padmasana forms an ideal stable base for sitting for longer periods, but unfortunately it also requires great flexibility. Apart from the fact that it is an extremely difficult posture to master, Padmasana is a symbolic posture and not really suitable for those aspiring to attain a high degree of proficiency on this path. It can be practiced for shorter periods of time to develop flexibility of the lower limbs.

Svastikasana: The Auspicious Pose

To sit in Svastikasana, bend the left leg and place the left foot alongside the right thigh. The sole of the left foot lies flat against the inside of the right thigh. Next, bend the right knee, and place the right foot gently between the left thigh and left calf. Finally, pull up the toes of your left foot between the right thigh and calf, so that the big toe is visible (Fig. 3.8).

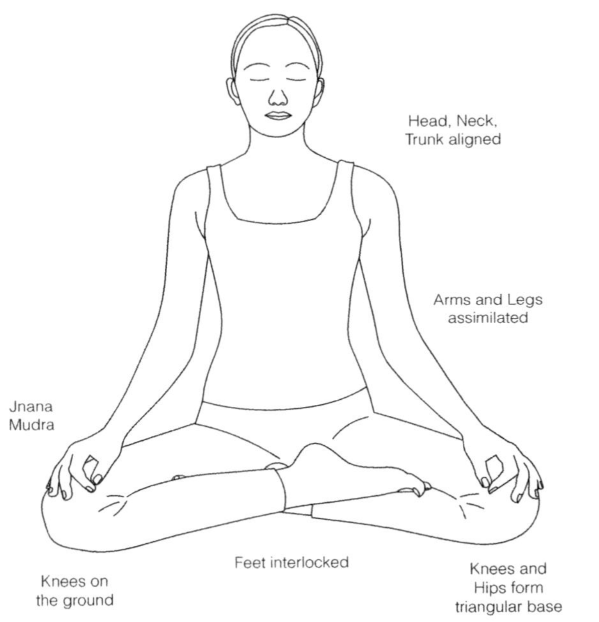

Figure 3.8 **Svastikasana**

In the Auspicious Pose or Svastikasana, head, neck and trunk are well aligned. If necessary, you can use layers of shawls (Fig. 3.1). The two knees and the base of the spine form the three corners of a triangle, so that the legs and hips make a stable, triangular base. The base is firm on the floor, giving the pose greater stability. The extremities are well assimilated and the feet are interlocked. If the ankle is resting directly on the floor, it may hurt, therefore always use a soft woolen blanket as a base. Keeping the feet interlocked may not appear to be important in the initial stages, but at a later stage it is very useful for those who aspire to practice *dhyana* or "deep meditation" and awaken kundalini.

Kundalini is an ancient word, a technical word from a forgotten science. Most people call kundalini a kind of energy, but they have no direct experience of this energy. The symbol of kundalini is the serpent. This is a symbol of our dark side or the deep unconscious mind. The energy of the unconscious mind is transmuted and raised to the conscious state of awareness. This is called kundalini in the ancient science of Tantra. If you are well prepared, it is possible to bring the unconscious mind into conscious awareness. As the unconscious mind comes forward, you may get agitated; keeping the feet interlocked prevents you from unconsciously jumping out of the posture. If you are sitting in Sukhasana or Ardha Padmasana, you can unconsciously slip out of your position very easily, but if you are sitting with the feet interlocked as in Padmasana or Svastikasana you cannot. If you are already comfortable sitting on the floor, you are not overweight and have no injuries then it is worth the effort to master Svastikasana. It is one of the easiest as well as one of the best positions for breathing exercises, pranayama and eventually dhyana.

You can use shawls to support the knees but all these props should be used only in the short-term. Props used over an extended period of time are not useful; they create dependency and do not really make the practitioner more flexible. In this case it is better to sit on the chair or in Sukhasana as well as practice asanas that promote flexibility.

While trying to master Svastikasana you may experience cramps occasionally and may want to stretch your legs or shift into Sukhasana. However, continuous movement or changes in the posture are not very useful. If you do this all the time, you will never develop the habit of sitting still. Every time you stretch your legs or change your posture, you come back to the body level, preventing yourself from having a deeper experience of the practice. It is important to sit for progressively longer sessions in Svastikasana without movement. To facilitate this, you need to practice a few joints and glands loosening exercises and asanas that develop flexibility of the body, keeping in mind that an undue emphasis on body culture is not required. You can practice loosening exercises such as ankle rotation, Vajrasana, Padmasana or any other asana, which will develop the flexibility of the ankles and knees. These will prevent cramps and discomfort. If you skip the loosening exercises or not do enough, you will be torturing yourself, creating tension in the body and nervous system. This is not useful for progress in pranayama. A more active lifestyle, for instance, daily walks and sports will also improve overall circulation in the body and prevent cramps.

Often people cannot sit in meditative postures because they are overweight. This problem can only be solved by losing weight through change in diet and lifestyle.

Siddhasana: The Accomplished Pose

In Siddhasana, the left heel is placed at the perineum, between the anus and the genitals. The right heel is placed at the pubic bone above the organ of generation. The feet and legs are arranged so that the ankle joints are in one line or touch each other. The toes of the right foot are placed between the left thigh and calf so that only the big toe is visible; the toes of the left foot are pulled up between the right thigh and calf so that the big toe is visible (Fig. 3.9).

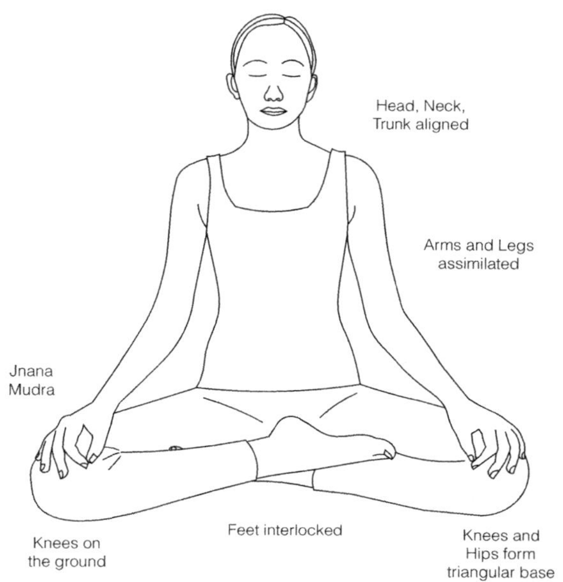

Figure 3.9 **Siddhasana**

The triangular base formed by the knees and the hips in Siddhasana is not as wide as in Svastikasana. The knees move closer inward and the heels under the body. Svastikasana naturally leads to Siddhasana.

Siddhasana is suitable for both men as well as women. However, women may find it uncomfortable for longer periods of time. Women may prefer Svastikasana for this reason.

What is the Best Posture for me?

Siddhasana is a pose we should not try to force upon ourselves. When students force themselves to sit in this position, the body gets tense, the muscles of the back are strained, and the arms and shoulders become stiff. It is impossible to meditate if your entire body is tense. Do not force yourself into Siddhasana because you think it is more advanced than Svastikasana.

Asana	English Name	Head, Neck, Trunk aligned	Legs & Arms assimilated	Stable Base	Feet Inter-locked	Jnana Mudra
Maitri Asana	Friendship Pose	✓	✗	✗	✗	✓
Vajrasana	Thunderbolt	✓	✓	✗	✗	✓
Sukhasana	Easy Pose	✓	✓	✗	✗	✓
Ardha Padmasana	Half Lotus	✓	✓	✓	✗	✓
Padmasana	Lotus	✓	✓	✓	✓	✓
Svastikasana	Auspicious Pose	✓	✓	✓	✓	✓
Siddhasana	Accomplished Pose	✓	✓	✓	✓	✓

Table 3.1 **Comparison of Seated Posture**

The best pose for you is the one that is most comfortable and in which you can sit for longer periods. If you have selected a pose in which you are not comfortable, then select an easier pose. If you are comfortable and can sit longer time in this position then this is the right pose for you. If you are using too many props, then go back to Maitri Asana or Sukhasana. After a few months of joints and glands loosening exercises and asanas you will be able to sit comfortably in Sukhasana or even Svastikasana with the support of a few layers of shawls.

For those who want to do just a little bit for their well-being, it is fine to sit in Maitri Asana or in Sukhasana for a short period of time. If you really aspire to master pranayama and eventually dhyana, practice systematically until you are able to sit comfortably in Svastikasana for a longer period of time. Then, it might happen quite naturally and effortlessly that one day you slip into Siddhasana.

Q&A

Question: Is it healthy to sit for long in a meditative posture? Isn't this encouraging a passive and sedentary lifestyle?

Answer: Meditative postures are quite different from sitting around on chairs and sofas. They have many positive benefits. However, if you already lead a sedentary lifestyle even these positive benefits may not be enough. You need to compensate for the lack of movement.

Traditionally it is said, that the sitting to movement ratio should be 1:4. This means, if you sit in a meditative posture for an hour every day, you also need to be active for four hours that day. This includes all kinds of movement and activity in the house and workplace, such as household chores, walking up and down steps, etc. To counterbalance our extreme sedentary lifestyle, it is important to consciously go for brisk walks, jogging, swimming or any other form of exercise.

Chapter 4

BASIC BREATHING TECHNIQUES

Having overcome the initial obstacles, finally you start practicing real breathing techniques only to discover: they are not so basic after all. These practices will take you from fifteen breaths per minute to one breath per minute. If you achieve this in less than a year, you have every reason to congratulate yourself.

Before you start any other breathing exercises, equal, diaphragmatic breathing must be mastered. Practicing other breathing practices without establishing equal, diaphragmatic breathing can damage the pranic vehicles. If the foundation is faulty, the entire building can collapse.

Order of Practice

Once you have established natural and effortless diaphragmatic breathing you can start practicing Equal Breathing, Rechaka or 2:1 Breathing, Kapalabhati, Bhastrika, Ujjayi and Bhramari. There is no rigid order. It is best to do these in consultation with an experienced guide. If you do not have a guide, you can practice the breathing exercises in the order that they are explained in. When you learn to play a musical instrument, you have to start by learning the octaves and playing simple compositions. That is the most basic step in music. Creating your own compositions of music requires a high order of mastery. The order of exercises and practices is akin to the notes of a musical composition. This order has been determined by experience to work well for all. Change in this order of practice is only necessary at a much higher level of practice when the practitioner is very sensitive to the subtle energies and wants to harmonize the different subtle energies.

The Most Important Step: Check the Base Count

The average person has a short and uneven breath. Such a person may breathe in 4 seconds and breathe out 3 seconds. In fact, the breath may be as short as 3 seconds in and 2 seconds out.

If we take the average breath of a person to be 2 seconds in and 2 seconds out, then such a person breathes at the rate of 15 breaths per minute.

Before you start breathing exercises you need to check your base count. The base count is the capacity of your exhalation and inhalation and you must always go with it. This is the most fundamental step and you cannot proceed without this.

The counting method is recommended because it does not encourage a dependency on any external objects such as a watch. Count silently in the mind. Count so that 1 count is equal to 1 second.

Check your breath at different times of the day. You may notice differences in the counts, depending on the time of the day, degree of tiredness and your emotional state. Accept the most common count as the base to start from.

Guiding Principle

Place your finger in front of your nostrils and feel your breath. Count the length of both, the exhalation as well as the inhalation. This is the base count.

Equal Breathing

Before you start Equal Breathing you should have already established point 1 of the 7 Step Program. This means you should have natural and effortless diaphragmatic breathing at all times of the day. In fact, Equal Breathing is the same as even, diaphragmatic breathing, but now you learn to use counts, to refine your breath and elongate it. The seated position allows for the finer study of the irregularities in the breath and correction of the same.

Variation 1: With Counts

Let us assume your natural breath count is: 4 seconds in, 3 seconds out. Take the lower count, in this case 3 seconds, as the base count.

Sit in your chosen meditative posture and do this practice silently. Breathe in 3 seconds and breathe out 3 seconds. This is 1 breath. Do this 10 times. This is 1 round. After a round, breathe normally for a couple of moments. Take the time between rounds to come back to your normal breathing. This may not seem to make a difference initially, but as you increase the number of counts, you will find these short breaks of normal breathing useful. Do another 2 rounds, remembering to take a break, and breathe normally between the rounds.

While you practice Equal Breathing observe your breath for the following irregularities: jerky breath, noisy breath and extended pauses. These are Steps 3–5 of the 7 Step Program. Consciously smooth out these irregularities.

Elongating the breath in Equal Breathing

Gradually increasing the counts will help establish Step 6 of the 7 Step Program leading to an equal, elongated breath.

If you started with the base count of 3 seconds out and 3 seconds in, then after two weeks increase the counts to 4 seconds out and 4 seconds in. Do 3 rounds of 10 breaths each. After another two weeks, increase the counts to 6 seconds out and 6 seconds in. Once again do 3 rounds of 10 breaths each.

Keep increasing the counts by 2 seconds every two weeks, until you reach 30 seconds out and 30 seconds in. That means 1 breath per minute. You will have achieved this gradually and gently over 7–8 months (Table 4.1). This gradual increase in counts is important so as not to damage the finer tissues of the lungs.

Start slowly by watching your capacity, slowly expanding the same. It is not possible to achieve this in a week or in a month. If you use force, you will hurt the finer tissues of your lungs. Take at least six months to master the process of breath elongation. At the end of 7–8 months you will be on the threshold of Step 7 and beginning to understand, experience and eventually gain mastery over prana itself.

This table shows how one can gradually increase breath counts. This is only a suggestion. In this plan the elongated breath is mastered over a period of 30 weeks, i.e. between 7–8 months.

Do not exceed your capacity! If necessary go back to a lower count or spend more than two weeks with a breath count.

Week	Breath Count
1–2	3
3–4	4
5–6	6
7–8	8
9–10	10
11–12	12
13–14	14
15–16	16
17–18	18
19–20	20
21–22	22
23–24	24
25–26	26
27–28	28
29–30	30

Table 4.1 **Equal Breathing**

Variation 2: Without Counts

You may notice that counting silently somehow disturbs the flow of the breath and makes it jerky. You may notice that due to counting there are unconscious pauses between exhalation and inhalation. In the method without counting you will be able to devote your attention to the finer aspects of the breath. There are two variations of this.

In the seated position

Sit in a meditative posture. Let your attention travel from the crown of the head to the base of the spine while exhaling and then let your attention travel from the base of the spine to the crown of the head while inhaling (Fig. 4.1). You are using the body to measure the length of exhalation and inhalation.

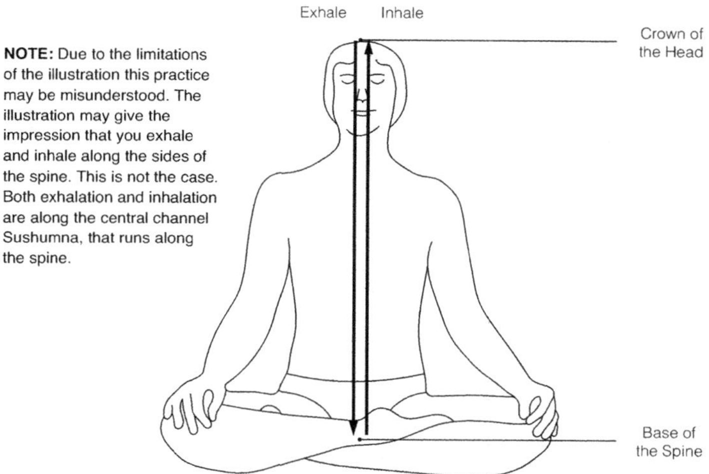

Figure 4.1 **Equal Breathing – Seated Position**

This exercise helps to establish and maintain the equal breath without counting and you can focus on allowing the breath to become smooth, silent and remove extended pauses.

In the supine position

Lie in Shavasana and breathe out from the crown of the head to the tip of the toes and breathe in from the tip of the toes to the crown of the head (Fig. 4.2). Once again you are using your own body to measure the length of exhalation and inhalation.

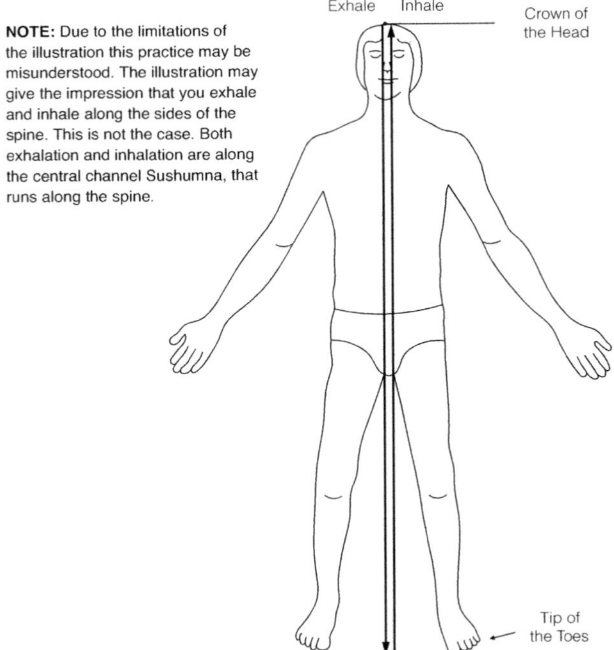

Figure 4.2 **Equal Breathing – Supine Position**

Shavasana is a very comfortable position to practice Equal Breathing. The supine position also allows you to elongate the exhalation and the inhalation. You may use this position if you are sure that you will not fall asleep while practicing. Falling asleep repeatedly during practice means that the mind will learn to use the technique to fall asleep. It is important to train the mind not to fall asleep during practice. Therefore, do not practice Equal Breathing in Shavasana when you are tired or sleepy. The best time to practice Equal Breathing in Shavasana is when you are well rested and alert, for instance, in the morning after a good night's sleep.

Rechaka or 2:1 Breathing

Before you start Rechaka you should have already established Step 1 of the 7 Step Program and should have natural and effortless diaphragmatic breathing at all times of the day. In 2:1 Breathing, known as Rechaka, the exhalation is twice the length that of the inhalation. Breathing out a greater volume of air than you are breathing in, releases the old air from your lungs.

Variation 1: With Counts

Sit in your chosen meditative posture and do this practice silently.

As with Equal Breathing, the fundamental step for Rechaka is checking your base count. Let us assume your natural base count is: 2 seconds in, 3 seconds out. Take the lower count, in this case 2 seconds. Breathe out 4 seconds and breathe in 2 seconds. This is 1 breath. Do this 10 times. This is 1 round. Do this consciously. After a round breathe normally. Take the time between rounds to come back to your normal breathing. This may not seem to make a difference initially, but as you increase the counts, you will find these short breaks of normal breathing useful. Do another 2 rounds, remembering to take a break and breathe normally between the rounds. Do this as part of your daily practice for about four weeks.

TIP: Always start breathing exercises with exhalation.

Elongating the breath in Rechaka

After about four weeks of practicing 2:1 Breathing increase the counts to 6 seconds out and 3 seconds in. Do 3 rounds of 10 breaths each. After another two weeks, increase the counts to 8 seconds out and 4 seconds in. Once again do 3 rounds of 10 breaths each.

Keep increasing the counts every second week, until you reach 30 seconds out and 15 seconds in. You will achieve this gradually and gently over 7–8 months (Table 4.2).

This table shows how one can gradually increase breath counts. This is only a suggestion. In this plan the elongated breath is mastered over a period of 30 weeks, i.e. between 7–8 months.

Do not exceed your capacity! If necessary go back to a lower count or spend more than two weeks with a breath count.

Week	Exhalation	Inhalation
1–4	4	2
5–6	6	3
7–8	8	4
9–10	10	5
11–12	12	6
13–14	14	7
15–16	16	8
17–18	18	9
19–20	20	10
21–22	22	11
23–24	24	12
25–26	26	13
27–28	28	14
29–30	30	15

Table 4.2 **Rechaka – 2:1 Breathing**

In the initial stages you may notice that you can exhale double the counts quite easily. However, as the counts increase, you will notice that you are reaching your limit. There is simply no more air to breathe out. At this point you must master the breathing apparatus so that the exhalation is slower than the inhalation. The very process of slow, smooth exhalation relaxes the entire body and the mind becomes calm and alert.

Variation 2: Without counts

After you have integrated 2:1 Breathing with counts in your practice, you may notice that counting somehow disturbs the flow of the breath and makes it jerky. You may also notice that the breath is noisy and that there are unconscious extended pauses between inhalation and exhalation. In the method without counting you will be able to devote your attention to the finer aspects of the breath.

In the seated position

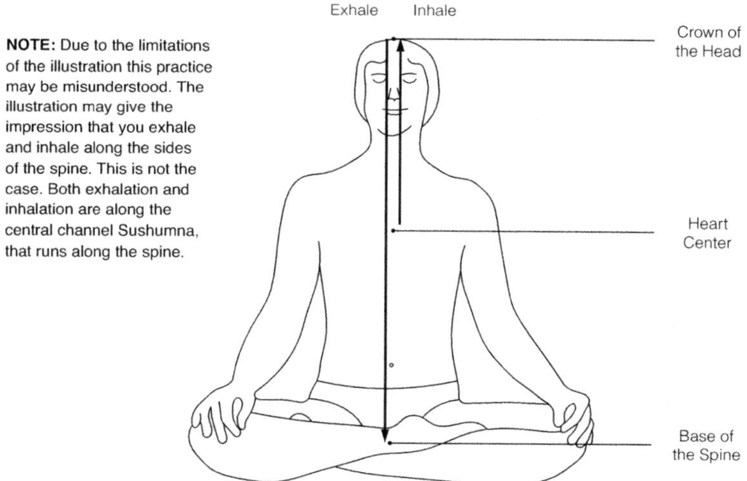

Figure 4.3 **Rechaka without Counting – Seated Position**

Sit in a meditative posture. Allow the attention to travel from the crown of the head to the base of the spine while exhaling. Let the attention travel from the heart center to the crown of the head while inhaling (Fig. 4.3). This makes the length of exhalation approximately double that of the inhalation.

In the supine position

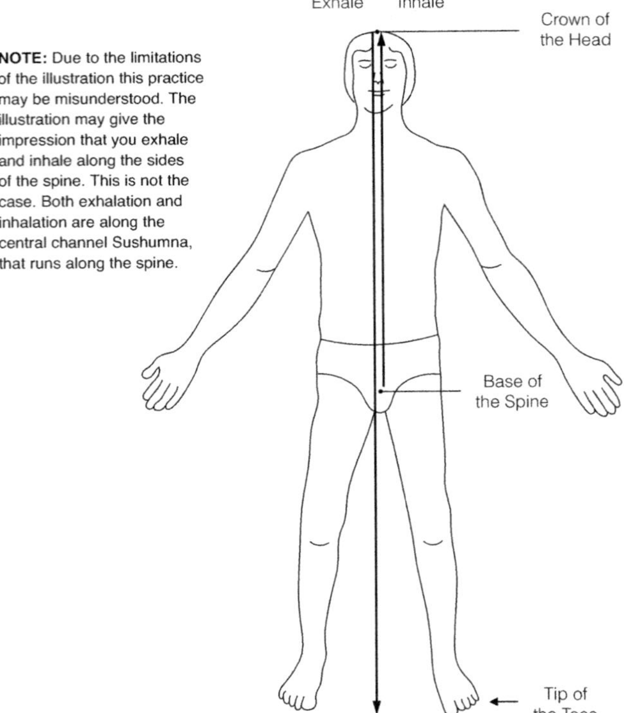

Figure 4.4 **Rechaka without Counting – Supine Position**

Another method is to lie down in Shavasana and breathe out as you let the attention travel from the crown of the head to the tip of the toes and breathe in as you let the attention travel from the base of the spine to the crown of the head (Fig. 4.4). In this manner the length of the exhalation is double the length of the inhalation. In the method without counting you are able to devote your attention to the finer aspects of the breath. The supine position also allows you to elongate the exhalation and inhalation.

Kapalabhati

Kapalabhati means "makes the forehead shine." Kapalabhati is not only useful for cleansing the body of *kapha* or "phlegm," but also for purifying and energizing the *nadis* or subtle energy channels.

Sit with the head, neck and trunk aligned in your chosen meditative posture. Using the diaphragm and the abdominal muscles, quickly and forcefully expel the breath. This is followed by a slower and spontaneous inhalation as the abdominal muscles relax. Begin with 10 expulsions in rapid succession. This is 1 round. Do 3 rounds of 10 expulsions each.

The system should not be strained. Between each round, rest and allow the respiration to return to normal. This period of rest between rounds varies according to need. They may not seem to make a difference initially, but as you increase the expulsions, you will find these short breaks of normal breathing useful. Whilst practicing Kapalabhati pay attention to the abdominal muscles.

Increasing the number of expulsions

You can increase the number of expulsions by 10 every two weeks until you have reached 120 expulsions per round. This will take between 6–8 months (Table 4.3).

To make sure that your system is not strained, take short breaks between rounds.

Do not exceed your capacity!If necessary, go back to a lower number of expulsions per round or spend more than two weeks with the given number of expulsions.

Week	Expulsions per round	Week	Expulsions per round
1–4	10	17–18	70
5–8	20	19–20	80
9–10	30	21–22	90
11–12	40	23–24	100
13–14	50	25–26	110
15–16	60	27–28	120

Table 4.3 **Kapalabhati**

The speed with which one performs Kapalabhati should not be increased at the cost of technique. Beginning with 1 expulsion per second, the practice may be increased to 2 expulsions per second; 120 expulsions per minute is a good rate to maintain.

Bhastrika: The Bellows

Bhastra means "the bellows." In Bhastrika, the abdominal muscles move in an action similar to that of a blacksmith's bellows, churning up the fire in the body.

How to practice Bhastrika

Sit with the head, neck and trunk aligned in your chosen meditative posture. Inhale slowly until the abdomen is fully expanded and then exhale forcefully through the nostrils. This is followed by rapid, repeated and vigorous inhalations and exhalations. Begin slowly, picking up speed like a train. An exhalation and an inhalation together, make up 1 cycle. The cycles are to be repeated in rapid succession. Start with 10 cycles. This is 1 round. After 1 round breathe normally. Take the time between rounds to return to normal breathing. This may not seem to make a difference initially, but as you increase the cycles in each round, you will find these short breaks of normal breathing useful.

Increasing the number of cycles

Do 3 rounds of 10 cycles each for three weeks. Then increase the number of cycles to 20 for another three weeks.

Bhastrika churns up large amounts of energy. Short breaks between rounds allow the energy to be integrated.

Do not exceed your capacity! If necessary, go back to a lower number of cycles per round or spend more than one week with the given number of cycles per round.

Week	Cycles per Round
1–3	10
4–6	20
7	30
8	40
9	50
10	60
11	70
12	80
13	90
14	100
15	110
16	120
17	130
18	140
19	150
20	160
21	170
22	180
23	190
24	200
25	210
26	220
27	230
28	240

Table 4.4 **Bhastrika**

As you get more comfortable with Bhastrika, you can increase the number of cycles by 10 every week. At the end of seven months you will be doing 3 rounds of 240 cycles of Bhastrika (Table 4.4). This is only a suggestion. Everyone has a different capacity and it is important that you do not exert yourself.

Ujjayi

The word *Ujjayi* comes from *jaya*, "victory." Ujjayi calms down the nerves and the entire body experiences a great deal of vitality. Exhalation and inhalation are even, slow and deep in this practice.

The unique part about Ujjayi is that it takes place with a partially closed glottis. When you exhale, you make a "ha" sound. When you inhale, you feel the breath on the roof of the mouth; the inhalation is accompanied by a soft sibilant "sa." Ujjayi is a breathing practice with a sound included in it to intensify the breath. In Ujjayi, the emphasis remains on the sound and in order to do that, you need to focus on that part of the throat, called the glottis. The breath should be equal and the mouth should be closed throughout the practice.

During the practice of Ujjayi the mind is focused spatially at the glottis listening to the sound generated there. With every exhalation listen to the sound "ha"; it is similar to "hum." Listen to the sound "sa" with every inhalation. This is the sound of the breath; it is singing the mantra Hamsa. The mantra Hamsa is also known as Soham. They are one and the same. Thus, in Ujjayi you amplify the natural sound of your breath and listen to it. You are combining two subtle things: breath and sound. You are shifting slowly from breath to space and to sound. Traditionally, the example of a caterpillar is given. The caterpillar moves slowly and gradually to the next leaf. At some point, it is on both leaves: partially on the first leaf and partially on the second leaf. In Ujjayi the breath is the first leaf and your mind is moving toward the second leaf, which is space. This is a transition. The mind is focused on the sound produced at the glottis until you eventually forget the space around the throat, and just listen to the sound, transitioning from space to sound. This is a very fine breathing practice and it prepares you for dhyana.

Bhramari

Bhramari comes from the Sanskrit word "bee." Besides making honey, bees make a wonderful humming sound like "hum." Does that sound familiar? It is the mantra Om or more accurately Aum.

Exhale, producing a humming sound without opening your mouth or moving your lips. Inhale naturally without any sound. Do the exhalation and inhalation for a couple of minutes. By now, you should have got the feel for the length of the breath and even though you do not count, the length of the exhalation and the inhalation should be more or less equal.

Initially, you may be more with the breath but as you get comfortable with the practice you can listen to the sound vibrating in your head. You do not need to close the glottis for Bhramari. Like Ujjayi, Bhramari uses the same caterpillar principle of moving from breath to the sound.

Breathing and One-pointedness

At how many places can you hold your attention simultaneously? Can anyone possibly focus on all these points at the same time: diaphragm, chest, glottis and sound? We need to unlearn one aspect of modern life, that is, allowing the mind to jump between multiple points of focus.

In the yogic process, you are learning to drop the many, keeping the mind focused like a laser beam. You do not want your energy to be dissipated. If your mind is on many different objects, trying to "multitask," then it is shifting from one thing to another constantly and rapidly. This is a divided and scattered mind. On the day you spend your time engaged in many different activities for short periods of time, you feel totally exhausted because the scattered mind dissipates your energy. To achieve something you need to be focused.

Find the focal point of a practice and try to stay with it. In Ujjayi, your focus is at the glottis. You have already established diaphragmatic breathing, so you do not need to focus the mind on the breathing apparatus anymore. Allow your attention to be at the glottis, at the top of the throat, and with time, as you become more proficient in the practice, you will experience yourself just being with the sound, "ham" and "sa." The same is true for Bhramari.

Purpose of Breathing Exercises and Pranayama

Through the practice of these breathing exercises, you will achieve multiple goals:

1. You will study your own breathing habits and correct the unhealthy breathing patterns.
2. You will remove the finer and subtler flaws in your breathing habits. This will expand your awareness to a subtler and finer level of consciousness than experienced in day to day reality.
3. You will remove wastes and toxins from your body, through Rechaka and cleansing practices like Kapalabhati, which emphasize exhalation. This rids the body of old air that is trapped in the lungs and expands the capacity of the chest.
4. You will energize your body by oxygenating the blood and not allowing this energy to be dissipated again, thus preparing the mind for advanced practices. This energy creates a certain pressure in the system and can be used to focus the mind.

5. You will notice the connection between thoughts, the breath and the body, expanding your self-awareness of mind and body, creating the perfect foundation for understanding the purpose of life.
6. All the above will bring with them many benefits in overall health and well-being and prepare you for pranayama.

Q&A

Question: Step 3 of the 7 Step Program is to have a silent breath. How can I do that with Kapalabhati, Bhastrika, Ujjayi and Bhramari?

Answer: Indeed, it is true that one of the points in the 7 Step Program is to establish a silent breath. The four practices Kapalabhati, Bhastrika, Ujjayi and Bhramari are exceptions. There is a sound in these breathing exercises but the sound is made consciously. In the other breathing exercises, we seek to eliminate the unconscious sounds.

Silent breathing aids in establishing a natural and effortless diaphragmatic breath that is also smooth and subtle. The silent breath is important for all the variations of Equal Breathing and 2:1 Breathing as well as in other practices to be explained in the following chapters, since a noisy breath can neither be subtle nor can it be elongated effectively.

Question: I get breathless when I practice Equal Breathing and Rechaka over 8 counts. Am I doing something wrong?

Answer: If you are following the 7–8 months plan then you should not experience breathlessness. The 7–8 months plan steadily and gently elongates the breath and helps to increase your breathing capacity over time. If you are not following this plan and have the ambition to achieve your target in less time, then it is possible that you are creating a lot of pressure to perform. In this case, the lungs are not able to keep up with your ambition. It is best you go back to doing fewer counts. Consistently pushing yourself beyond your capacity can damage the finer tissues of the lungs and disturb the pranic vehicles.

If you are following the 7–8 months plan and still feeling breathless, there could be three possible causes:

The first is that you have a respiratory disorder. In this case, consult a doctor. In case of acute or chronic respiratory problems never practice breathing exercises without the guidance of an experienced teacher or before consulting a doctor.

The second cause could be poor lung capacity. Those who live a sedentary lifestyle often have poor lung capacity. This can be improved with regular exercise such as brisk walking, swimming, cycling and other physical activities. Besides this, you can slow down the 7–8 months plan. Move to a higher count only when you are absolutely comfortable; you may then require a year or even two, to achieve the set target of 30 seconds exhalation and 30 seconds inhalation.

The third cause could be incorrect technique. As you start to elongate your breath, you do two things over time: increase lung capacity as well as slow down the breathing. Once the lung capacity has reached the maximum you cannot inhale more air. Therefore, the trick is to breathe slowly. You slow down the breath so that the volume of air intake is stretched over a longer period of time.

Question: Kapalabhati and Bhastrika involve rapid breathing. Does this not agitate the mind and nervous system?

Answer: The purpose of Kapalabhati is to release wastes from the respiratory system. Bhastrika churns up energy in the solar plexus. Both the techniques use the diaphragm and the breathing is rhythmic. Most important, the breathing is conscious and done with complete awareness for a brief period of time as opposed to unconscious breathing patterns that are unrhythmic and shallow over a long period of time. It is shallow, unrhythmic breathing, over a long period of time, that causes a permanent state of stress in the body and is harmful to the body.

Kapalabhati and Bhastrika should not be practiced more than four times a day. Never exceed your limits.

Question: I feel light and heady after breathing exercises, almost like I am floating. Is this a direct experience of Adi Prana?

Answer: Breathing exercises remove wastes such as carbon dioxide and increase the intake of oxygen. The increased oxygenation reflects in a sense of well-being. If you continue the breathing exercises for a longer time with elongated breath, you will also feel light and heady, a feeling you might describe as floating. While this may be pleasant, this is neither the purification of the nadis nor the direct experience of Adi Prana.

Breathing exercises are like floating on the surface of a lake: they are superficial. While pranayama is like diving deep underwater. The water, in this case, is prana the life element; you can breathe it and it will not kill you. In fact, Adi Prana has the quality of life and will enliven you. It will make you contemplative and extremely joyous. It will bring with it a flood of insights and wisdom. This seems to be the closest you will get to understanding Adi Prana, until you experience it for yourself.

Question: You have mentioned two ways of measuring the length of the breath: one is counting and the other is using the spine or the length of the body as a measure. I listen to my heart beats and use the number of heart beats to keep count. Is this an acceptable method?

Answer: It is not always easy to listen to the heart beats without placing your hand on the heart. If this is the case, you will not be completely relaxed. Holding the hand in this position will get uncomfortable after a while. Even if the surroundings are quiet and you have developed a sharp inner ear to listen to the heart beats, the heart beats are not always constant. They may slow down as the breath elongates. They may also slow down in breathing exercises such as 2:1 Breathing. On the other hand, the heart might beat more rapidly during Bhastrika and Kapalabhati. Thus, heart beats are not a reliable measure of time.

Using the heart beats to measure the length of the breath does not bring any added advantage with it, since you still have to keep count of the heart beats. You cannot give up counting altogether. Listening to the heart beats also keeps you spatially focused on the heart center. This center may not be suitable for everyone.

However, the most important reason why heart beats are not suitable for measuring the length of the breath is that this method does not simultaneously train the mind to move along the spine and train the reversal of energy flow. Understanding and practicing the process of reversing and redirecting the flow of energy is an absolute must to master advanced pranayama. You will be introduced to the process of energy reversal in the advanced section of this book.

Chapter 5

SVARODAYA, THE MYSTICAL SCIENCE OF BREATH

Learning to churn up the subtle energy and integrating it requires one-pointedness. The feminine and masculine energies are harmonized; the divided mind and body are brought into balance. Practice regularly and you are well on your way to become a master of the fine breath and even finer mind.

When modern medicine confronted ancient yogic science in the nineteenth century, the medical community was quick to point out that there is no such thing as nadis and *chakras* in the body. To demonstrate this, they dissected the body. However, astute observers did notice the parallels between the nadis and the different nerves in the body; they also observed that the location of the *chakras* corresponded with important glands and ganglia.

According to yogic literature there are over 72,000 nadis. It is important to understand that nadis are not nerves, but the subtler counterpart of the nerves. For our purposes only three nadis are of significance: ida, pingala and sushumna. Both ida and pingala run along the spine. Both originate at the base of the spine. According to some texts they alternate from right to left and right again; according to other texts they run along the side of the spine in a bow form. The central channel or nadi that travels along the spine is known as sushumna. This is the most important of all nadis.

While ida and pingala open alternately in healthy persons, sushumna is barely open during the transition from ida to pingala and back. Sushumna generally remains blocked. The purpose of pranayama practices is to consciously open the central channel sushumna.

What is Anuloma Viloma?

One of the most important practices is known as *Anuloma Viloma*. *Loma* means "hair" and *anu* is "in the direction of the hair." *Vi* is a prefix that indicates "against the direction." This expression probably owes its origin to the Ayurvedic practice of massaging in the direction and against the direction of body hair to invigorate the body energy. *Anuloma* means "in the natural direction" and *Viloma* means "in the opposite direction." This principle of invigorating the body is also used with the breath.

The normal flow of energy is downward from the crown of the head to the base of the spine. Pranayama practices seek to reverse the energy flow and lead the flow upward to the higher centers of consciousness.

Imagine that the energy channel is like a river meandering through the plains and you are rowing a boat. Anyone who has rowed a boat knows it is easy to row with the current but a great deal of effort is required to row against the flow of the current. Now imagine that this is not just a river in the plains but in the mountains and you are trying to row upstream to the source of the river. You can well imagine that this is extremely challenging, if not impossible, since the river is rushing downhill. Yet incredibly enough this is exactly what you want to achieve.

Guiding Principle

Open the Sushumna and reverse the flow of energy.

Coming back to the river and boat example: if you start from the right bank to row upstream to the source of the river, the current will force you to row close to the right bank. To confront the full force of the powerful current means you will be completely washed away. In this manner you will be able to go upstream to the source of the river with a great deal of effort, training, skill, alertness and lots of patience. The practice of Anuloma Viloma, seeks to gently reverse the energy flow by alternating the flow of the breath from one nostril to the other, bring them into balance, to open sushumna and lead the energy upward to the crown of the head.

With the practice of Anuloma Viloma you are:

- purifying and energizing the pranic channels
- balancing both ida and pingala
- training to go against the downward flowing energy by alternately activating ida and pingala
- prepare for the opening of sushumna

Nadi Shodhanam: Alternate Breathing

Anuloma Viloma is also known as Nadi Shodhanam. *Shodhanam* comes from *shudh*, which means "to purify."

Once you have established natural diaphragmatic breathing, your breath is silent and smooth and you have also eliminated extended pauses, you are ready to start Nadi Shodhanam. You should have also elongated the breath and should be able to do it without counting. To do this practice with counting takes away from the main focus, which is the shifting of nostril flow. Before you start Nadi Shodhanam, you should have developed a feel of the equal breath. If you do not have a feel for the equal breath, then continue to do Equal Breathing without counting. Only when you have left the counting behind and have developed a feel for the equal breath, should you start Nadi Shodhanam.

There are different variations of Nadi Shodhanam, some of these are practiced with breath retention or Kumbhaka. However, Kumbhaka is not recommended in combination with Nadi Shodhanam. Kumbhaka is an advanced practice and there are other techniques that lead gently to Kumbhaka. You will learn these in Chapter 10 and Chapter 11.

For the purpose of mastering pranayama, there are three important variations of Nadi Shodhanam, all without breath retention. These three variations should be practiced and mastered in the same order they are explained. Nadi Shodhanam is generally practiced with the use of the fingers in a special manner called Vishnu Mudra. The method of Nadi Shodhanam with Vishnu Mudra is only a stepping stone to the advanced practice of Nadi Shodhanam without Vishnu Mudra. The method described here is the simplest and most comfortable. You do not need to use any other external aids.

How to practice Vishnu Mudra

Bend the forefinger and the middle finger of your right hand towards the palm. This is known as Vishnu Mudra (Fig. 5.1).

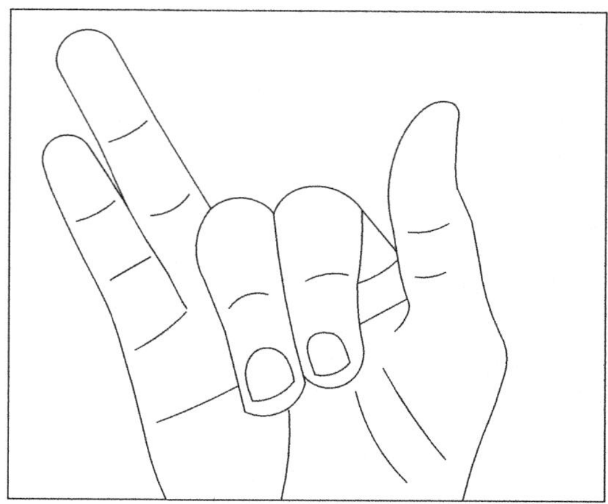

Figure 5.1 **Vishnu Mudra**

Use the right thumb to close the right nostril (Fig. 5.2). The ring finger and the little finger can be used to close the left nostril (Fig.5.3). When you apply Vishnu Mudra, you do not need to use any pressure, just a gentle touch is enough.

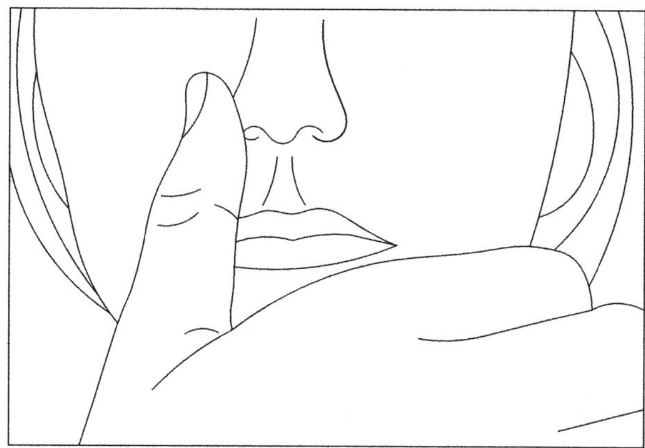

Figure 5.2 **Vishnu Mudra: Right Thumb closes Right Nostril**

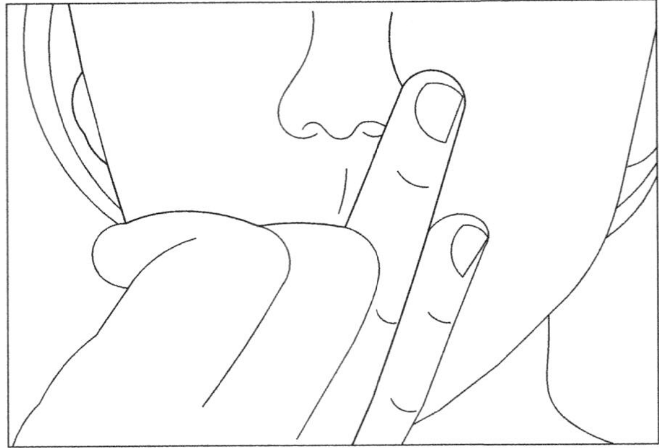

Figure 5.3 **Vishnu Mudra: Right Ring and Little Finger close Left Nostril**

There is a slightly different variation of Vishnu Mudra in which the forefinger and middle finger of the right hand are placed between the eyebrows. In this variation the thumb and ring finger are used to alternately open and close the nostrils. The arm must be held higher and it begins to ache after a while. There is no advantage to this method.

Base for Nadi Shodhanam

In the earlier breathing exercises you started with a base count. You do not need to keep counts now that you have developed a feel for the even and elongated breath. Yet, there is a base for this practice.

> **Guiding Principle**
>
> You need to find out, which is the active nostril and which is the passive nostril. This is the base for Nadi Shodhanam. Before you start this practice, put your forefinger below your nostrils and test which nostril is active.

Generally, one nostril is dominant at any given time. The flow shifts naturally from left to right and right to left. This cycle is between 60–120 minutes long. This breathing cycle was discovered empirically by the ancient sages. These observations were handed down and validated by subsequent generations of practitioners. During the transition period when there is a shift, it may feel as though both are active for a brief period. The sushumna is barely open during this transition. An astute observer may still notice that one nostril flows slightly more freely than the other, making it the active nostril.

Experiment

Study your breath over a longer period of time and you will notice that generally only one nostril is active. Use the given table (Table 5.1) to record your observations.

Breath & Time

Day	Morning Hours					Afternoon Hours					Evening Hours				
	8	9	10	11	12	1	2	3	4	5	6	7	8	9	10
1															
2															
3															

How to use the chart: Observe your breath for at least three days. Set alarms on your mobile for every hour. At every hour, hold your forefinger before your nostrils and observe which nostril is flowing freely. This is the active nostril. Make a note of the active nostril in the appropriate column. If the left nostril is flowing freely, mark the box with L. If the right nostril is active, mark the box with R. If both nostrils seem to be flowing freely, then the breath is transitioning between the two nostrils. In this case, mark the box with T. As you continue observing, you may notice that even if both nostrils seem to be flowing, one is more dominant. This means the breath is transitioning. In this case, mark the box with TL, if the left nostril is slightly more dominant or TR, if the right nostril is slightly more dominant.

Breath & Emotions

Day	Morning Hours				Afternoon Hours				Evening Hours			
	10	Emotion	12	Emotion	3	Emotion	5	Emotion	8	Emotion	10	Emotion
4												
5												
6												

How to use the chart: Observe your breath for another three days. Set alarms on your mobile for the scheduled hours. Observe your breath and make a note of the active nostril. Now find a word or two to describe the state of your mind at that point of time: creative, dynamic, focused, joyous, excited, contemplative, analytical, logical, happy, calm, balanced, dull, sad, nervous, tense or angry. Study the relationship between the breath and emotions. You may notice a pattern.

Table 5.1 **Breath Observation**

To download the above table, scan the QR code:

How to practice Nadi Shodhanam

There are three variations of Nadi Shodhanam. Most practitioners know either Variation 1 or Variation 2. However, it is important to learn all three variations and practice them in the given sequence.

Nadi Shodanam Variation 1

Sit in a meditative pose. Determine which nostril is active. Allow the eyes to be gently closed. Use Vishnu Mudra to close the nostrils in alternation. Always use the right thumb to close the right nostril (Fig. 5.2) and the right ring finger and little finger to gently close the left nostril (Fig. 5.3).

Gently close the passive nostril and exhale smoothly through the active nostril. At the end of the exhalation, close the active nostril, release the passive nostril, and inhale slowly through the passive nostril. This is 1 cycle. The duration of the inhalation and exhalation should be equal. The inhalation and exhalation should be slow, smooth and silent. There should be no pauses. Do 2 more cycles.

At the end of the third inhalation through the passive nostril, exhale through the same nostril keeping the active nostril closed. When this exhalation is complete, close the passive nostril and then open the active one, inhaling through the active nostril. This is 1 cycle. Repeat this 2 more times, exhaling through the passive and inhaling through the active. This is 1 set of Nadi Shodhanam Variation 1 (Fig. 5.4). You will find the diagram very useful and easy to follow.

You can rest your hands on the knees in Jnana Mudra and breathe normally through both nostrils for 5–10 seconds before you start a set of Variation 2. Take the time to return to your normal breathing. This may not make a difference initially, but as you elongate your breath, you will find this little break very useful.

The duration of the inhalation and exhalation should be equal but you need not count. Counting makes this practice difficult. You need to remember which nostril is active and which is passive, and keep shifting your attention between the two nostrils. This already requires a high degree of attention. If you are going to include counting and coordinate this with breath retention or breath suspension, you will be overwhelmed. By the time you start practicing Nadi Shodhanam you should have got a feel for an equal breath, so that you can focus entirely on shifting your attention from one nostril to the other.

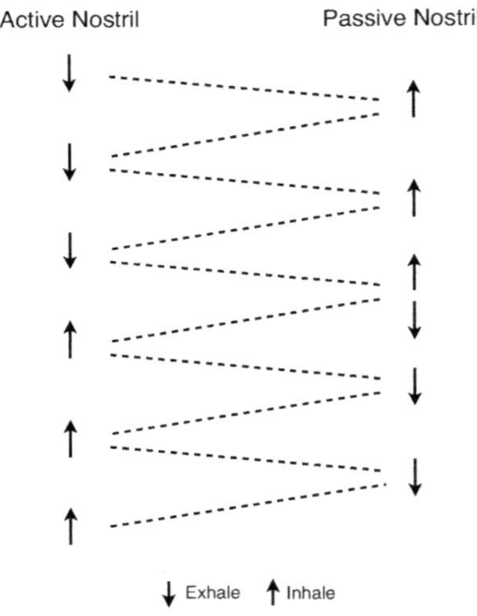

Figure 5.4 **Nadi Shodhanam – Variation 1**

Nadi Shodhanam Variation 2

Breathe out from the active nostril and breathe in again from the same nostril. Now shift your attention to your passive nostril. Breathe out from the passive nostril and breathe in from the same nostril. This is 1 cycle. Repeat the cycle 2 more times. This is 1 set (Fig. 5.5).

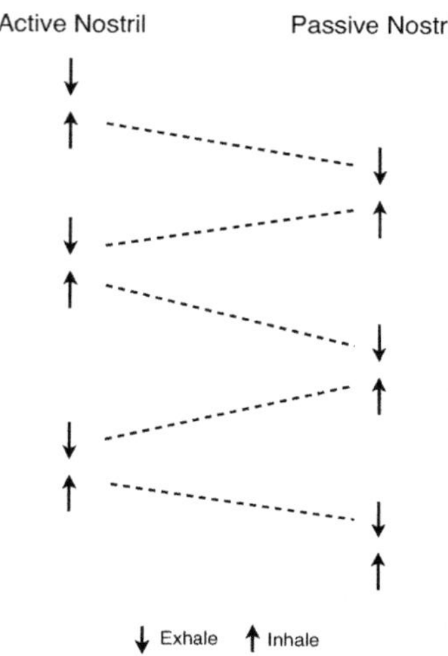

Figure 5.5 **Nadi Shodhanam – Variation 2**

TIP: Start all Nadi Shodhanam variations by exhaling from the active nostril.

Nadi Shodhanam Variation 3

Focus your attention at the active nostril. Exhale and inhale through the active nostril. This is 1 cycle. Repeat 2 more times. Shift your attention to the passive nostril. Exhale and inhale through the passive nostril. This is 1 cycle. Repeat 2 more times. This is 1 set of Variation 3 (Fig. 5.6).

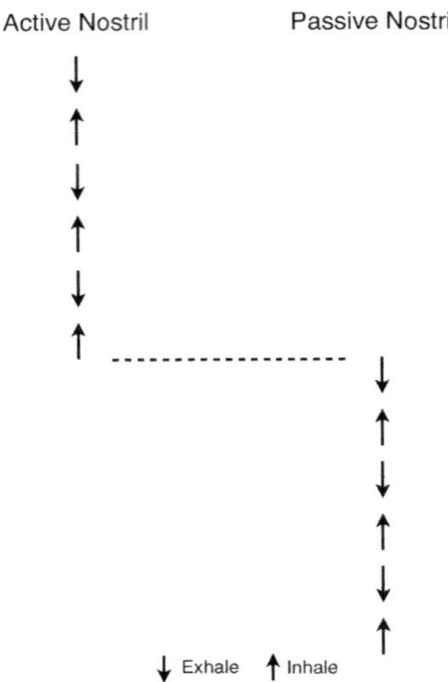

Figure 5.6 **Nadi Shodhanam – Variation 3**

Understanding the Three Variations of Nadi Shodhanam

Study the diagrams of the three different variations and you will notice that the shifting of attention from one nostril to the other is the most in Variation 1. For example, if the length of exhalation and inhalation is 5 seconds or counts, then you are shifting your attention every 5 seconds.

In Variation 2 the movement from one nostril to the other decreases and in effect you allow your attention to rest longer at one point. For instance, if the length of exhalation and inhalation is 5 seconds then you are shifting your attention only every 10 seconds.

In Variation 3 the movement from one nostril to the other decreases further and you allow your attention to rest much longer at one point. For example, if the length of exhalation and inhalation is 5 seconds then in this variation you are shifting your attention only every 30 seconds. It is best to start with Nadi Shodhanam only after you have elongated your breath base count to 10 seconds. If you have elongated your breath and the base count of exhalation and inhalation is 10 seconds, then you shift your attention only once every 60 seconds in Variation 3.

In Variation 1 the mind moves rapidly from one point to the other. This is much like the normal state of the mind, which is multi-pointed. In Variation 2 the mind is trained to slow down this movement, which is why the practitioner perceives this variation as more difficult, even a little uncomfortable. In Variation 3 the practitioner is training his mind to stay still at one point. Thus, this order of practice trains the mind to slow down gradually.

TIP: Do all three variations in exactly this order to help the mind calm down.

The shifting of attention from the active nostril to the passive nostril requires your full awareness. In Nadi Shodhanam the practitioner is using the breath to slowly shift the attention to the mind, following the caterpillar and leaves principle. You train your mind gradually to locate a very fine and subtle focal point. In the initial practice of Diaphragmatic Breathing the mind was vaguely focused on the larger space of the diaphragm and abdomen. In most of the breathing exercises, the attention was located vaguely in the area of abdomen or nostrils. In Nadi Shodhanam the mind is trained to find a single point of focus alternately at the left and the right nostril and at the same time it is trained in one-pointedness. This is a critical aspect of the training.

Yogic literature often refers to the one-pointed mind or one-pointedness. The one-pointed mind focuses on one thing and only on that thing continuously. Having the breath as your focal point means, you are only with the breath. If you are leading a lifestyle that promotes multi-pointedness, you will not be able to sustain this because most of the time you are training multi-pointedness. You spend your time working and listening to music at the same time, eating and watching television, driving and talking on the mobile, cooking and texting your friends. That is why this step cannot be skipped or taken lightly; it will help in training one-pointedness. Possibly, this will be a new and difficult experience for you.

Why is it important to learn to shift the flow of air from one nostril to the other? To understand this you must dive into the ancient science of breath and prana.

The Science of Breath and Prana

Breath is one of the only aspects of the body, which is voluntary as well as involuntary. So you can use the breath as a handle to influence the nervous system and the brain.

Breath and the Pranavadins

Among the yogis were a special group of practitioners that studied the breath and its influence on the body, the mind and the nervous system. The science of breath and prana was perfected through empirical study by many generations of yogis in a direct lineage. These yogis are known as *pranavadins*; their science is known as *Svarodaya*. What these internal scientists discovered empirically thousands of years ago is only now being studied and understood by modern science.

Breath, Mind and Nadis

Ida, the moon is the feminine side and pingala, the sun is the masculine side.

Ida, related to the left side of the body, is responsible for artistic and visual abilities, imagination, musical and creative abilities, fantasy and 3-dimensional images, face and shape recognition, holistic thinking, insight and intuition. The lunar or the feminine side is the seat of non-verbal expression and emotions; it looks at the whole picture rather then the details.

Pingala, connected to the right side of the body, is related to analytical and rational thinking, logic, reasoning, language skills, numerical skills and verbal thinking. It is systematic, organized, and processes information in an analytical and sequential way. The solar or masculine side is the seat of strategic thinking and rules. It goes into details; it looks at the pieces of information first and then puts it together to get the whole picture (Fig. 5.7).

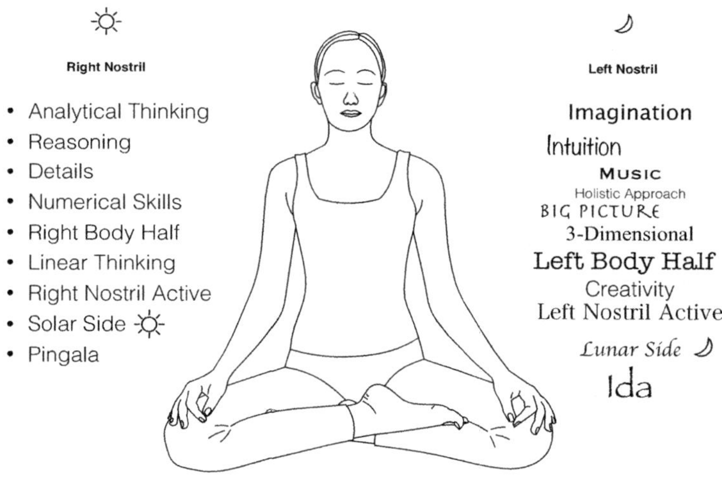

Figure 5.7 **Breath, Mind and Nadis**

The sympathetic and parasympathetic nervous systems correspond to the solar and lunar respectively. They can be considered to be positive and negative electric currents. The word "negative" is a balancing factor to the positive; it is not a pejorative. Understanding the lunar and solar sides as electric currents is a useful analogy. This relationship between the breath, the mind and the nervous system was already known to the ancient science of Tantra long before the birth of modern science.

There are two main universal principles: the feminine principle and the masculine principle. The observant practitioner sees these two principles everywhere. The world is a play of these two dualities of pleasure and pain, joy and sorrow, hot and cold, abundance and poverty, youth and old age, love and hate, good and evil, right and left, sun and moon, light and dark, conscious and unconscious, life and death. The pranavadin sees both these principles in the body and mind. Through empirical study he ascertains that the dualities that exist in the external world are reflected in the internal world and vice versa. The idea of the microcosm and macrocosm is a fundamental principle of this science. The softer and gentler feminine qualities have been overshadowed by the more dominant masculine qualities that are encouraged in most modern societies. We all have feminine qualities, but these are generally neglected to the detriment of our overall development. By bringing pingala and ida, that is, the masculine principle and feminine principle respectively into balance, the pranavadin seeks to go beyond the dualities.

The pranavadin is an observer par excellence. You too can be a pranavadin, if you learn to observe your breath, study its relationship to the mind and establish patterns between them. You may observe that at certain times of the day the left nostril is more dominant. You may enjoy creative and contemplative tasks during this period. If you observe that at certain times of the day, the right nostril is open, it is the perfect time for more active tasks or those requiring more analytical and logical thinking.

To be a pranavadin means studying your breath meticulously. Use the table and fill it in conscientiously (Table 5.1), so that you find the connection between the shift in your breathing cycle and the time of the day. After studying your breath for a few days answer the following questions:

- How often does the breath cycle change?
- Is the breath cycle regular?
- If so, how long is your breath cycle?

- Is there any particular time when the transitions seem to occur? Is there a particular time of the day when the left nostril and right brain is active?
- Which nostril is dominant in the morning when you wake up?
- Which nostril is flowing freely in the morning hours between 8 a.m.–12 noon?
- What kind of work do you like to do in the morning?
- Which nostril is dominant in the afternoon between 1 p.m.–5 p.m.?
- What do you like to do in the afternoons?
- Which nostril is open and active in the evening between 6 p.m.–10 p.m.?
- What do you like to do in the evenings?

You are now beginning to get a feel for the pranic science of Svarodaya. You may observe that a certain nostril is more dominant over a longer period of time. This indicates a fundamental imbalance. The excessive dominance of either side of the nostril indicates a disturbance in the pranic vehicle and leads to disease as well as personality disorders. One of the ways to work with this imbalance is with the daily practice of Nadi Shodhanam.

Dangers of Nadi Shodhanam

Nadi Shodhanam, also known as Anuloma Viloma, is extremely useful. It has many functions, such as:

- balancing the feminine and masculine sides of the body
- preparing the mind for advanced pranayama and dhyana
- slowing the movement of the mind
- training the mind to concentrate on a single point

However, incorrectly practiced Nadi Shodhanam can be harmful. Nadi Shodhanam should never be practiced with loud and forceful breathing. This disturbs the finer pranic energy.

Excessive interference in the natural breathing rhythm, such as forcefully attempting to change nostril flow to left side to do creative work is not recommended. This too can cause damage to the subtle pranic vehicles and can lead to headaches, mood swings and irritability. It is best to practice a single set of each variation of Nadi Shodhanam. You can practice these three sets up to four times daily.

Breath retention or breath suspension is also not useful in accompaniment with Nadi Shodhanam, primarily because Kumbhaka should occur naturally and effortlessly as a result of systematic breathing exercises and pranayama practices. Forcefully holding the breath is dangerous and not recommended.

To combine Nadi Shodhanam with physical movement is also not recommended. The mind is already occupied with the subtler focal point of the breath; it is counterproductive to give the mind additional focal points. The process of meditation goes from gross to subtle, therefore one should have left the body behind and should prepare for the subtler and direct observation of the mind itself.

MASTERING PRANAYAMA

Part 2: Advanced

"That pranayama which goes beyond the sphere of external and internal is the fourth pranayama."

Yoga Sutras II.51

Chapter 6

AN ANCIENT SECRET IS REVEALED

You always wanted to be in on a secret? That moment has arrived. A word of caution though: the difficulty lies not in the ability to practice the secret, but in the ability to accept it. Accept that it is possible and you will be soon saying, "Look, no hands!" Then you can tell one and all that you are an advanced practitioner.

The difference between breathing exercises and pranayama is that pranayama can be done mentally. Breathing exercises are important, but superficial. They prepare you to do pranayama. Through pranayama you can open sushumna nadi; through breathing exercises you cannot. Through pranayama you can also master Kumbhaka, the breathless state.

So far, you have prepared yourself for pranayama by correcting faulty breathing patterns and learning breathing exercises. Now we can focus on Step 7 by beginning to understand, experience and eventually attain mastery over prana itself.

Before you start pranayama you must have already established:

1. natural and effortless diaphragmatic breathing
2. even breathing, that is exhalation is equal to inhalation
3. silent breathing
4. smooth breathing, without jerkiness
5. elimination of extended pauses between exhalation and inhalation
6. the elongated breath, that is, increasing the length of exhalation and inhalation

By now you should be able to do all the three variations of Nadi Shodhanam without any external guidance. If that is the case, you are ready to explore how Nadi Shodhanam is done without Vishnu Mudra. Spend at least four weeks mastering all the three variations of Nadi Shodhanam with Vishnu Mudra before you attempt it without Vishnu Mudra.

The Secret to Mastering Pranayama

The great secret to mastering prana itself is learning to shift the flow of breath at will with the power of attention and without the use of fingers or any other external aids.

Learning to shift the nostril flow from the left to the right nostril and back is not an intellectual or analytical process. It only requires you to mentally observe. The very act of observing the breath at the space in front of the left or the right nostril activates that particular nostril. Even if the particular nostril is passive, by paying attention to it, it becomes active.

 **Guiding Principle**

Gently focus your attention at the left nostril and the left nostril will become active. Focus your attention at the right nostril and the right nostril will become active.

What seems impossible at first thought, is possible with daily practice over a longer period of time. While most practitioners need months to master this, the best of practitioners can master this in a matter of days. Understanding what prana is and acquiring a direct experience of it, is not possible without learning how to shift the flow of breath from one nostril to another mentally.

How to practice Nadi Shodhanam without Vishnu Mudra

Once you know the three variations of Nadi Shodhanam by heart and you do not need external aids such as oral or printed instructions to take you through the practice, you can drop Vishnu Mudra. You can focus the mind on shifting the flow of breath with the power of attention and eventually bring your breath function under your conscious control.

By now, you should feel comfortable in one of the traditional meditation postures. Sit with the head, neck and trunk in a straight line. Sit in your chosen meditative posture with your eyes closed and do this practice silently. You may sit in:

- Sukhasana, the Easy Pose
- Svastikasana, the Auspicious Pose
- Siddhasana, the Accomplished Pose

Determine which nostril is active by holding the forefinger in front of the nostrils. This is the base nostril. When you master Nadi Shodhanam without Vishnu Mudra, your awareness will become very sharp and you will be able to determine the base nostril, just by allowing your awareness to rest at the nostrils without using the finger.

Having determined the base nostril, allow the eyes to close gently. Let your hands rest in Jnana Mudra on your knees. Focus your attention on the space directly at the active nostril and exhale smoothly through it. At the end of the exhalation, shift your attention to the space just outside the passive nostril, and slowly inhale through the passive nostril (Fig. 6.1). This is 1 cycle. Do 2 more cycles.

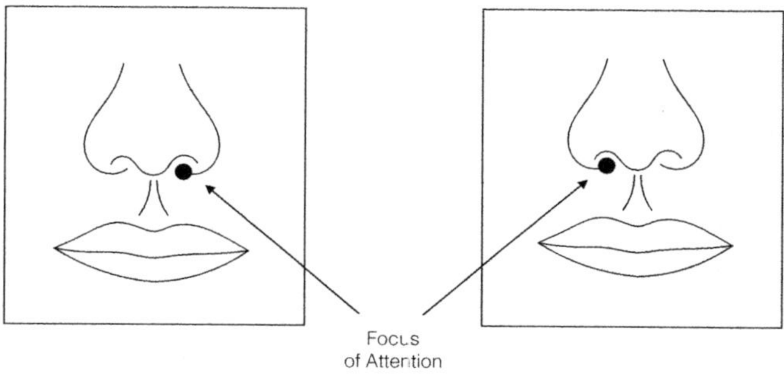

Figure 6.1 **Shifting Flow of Breath – RIGHT Technique**

At the end of the third inhalation through the passive nostril, exhale through the same nostril. When this exhalation is complete, shift your attention to the space just outside the active nostril and inhale through the active nostril. This is 1 cycle. Repeat this 2 more times, exhaling through the passive and inhaling through the active nostril. This is one set of Nadi Shodhanam Variation 1.

Exhale and inhale through both nostrils normally for a few moments before starting a set of Nadi Shodhanam Variation 2. Take the time between sets to come back to your normal breathing. By now you should have elongated your breath and this break between variations of normal breath is restful.

You can also practice Nadi Shodhanam Variation 3 without using Vishnu Mudra. By shifting your breath, you are training your attention to be one-pointed. Variation 3 is very important since this variation helps to open a passive nostril. It is the key to opening sushumna. Yet, it is important not to skip Variations 1 and 2. You may begin to feel restless or agitated if you start directly with Variation 3.

Important Tips

1. Learning to focus awareness on the space directly at the nostrils is a critical aspect of training that should not be ignored or skipped. This is the key to mastering pranayama.

There are teachers who combine many practices. They do breath retention and 2:1 Breathing with Nadi Shodhanam. These take your attention away from the main purpose, which is mastering the process of shifting your attention. There are already many things you need to master: you have to distinguish between the active nostril and the passive nostril, you have to shift your attention between these, and you have to do three different variations. This requires a lot of concentration. By adding either 2:1 Breathing or breath retention to this fine practice you take away the focus from shifting nostrils to keeping track of breath length once again.

2. You do not need to keep a count since you should already have a feel for a long, smooth and silent breath without extended pauses. When you drop Vishnu Mudra and the counting you may feel a bit lost initially, but you will soon begin to enjoy focusing on the breath without any disturbance of counting. It is only then that you may notice that the counting had caused very subtle jerks and pauses in the breath.

3. You will observe a tendency to visualize inhalation as a movement of breathing in and moving upward in the nostril. During exhalation you will notice the tendency to breathe out and visualize

the breath going down and out (Fig. 6.2). This is a wrong technique. Instead just shift your attention from one nostril to the other, spatially moving horizontally between the nostrils (Fig. 6.1).

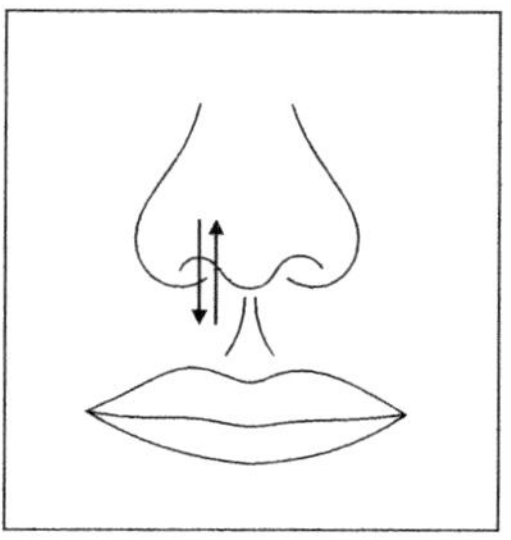

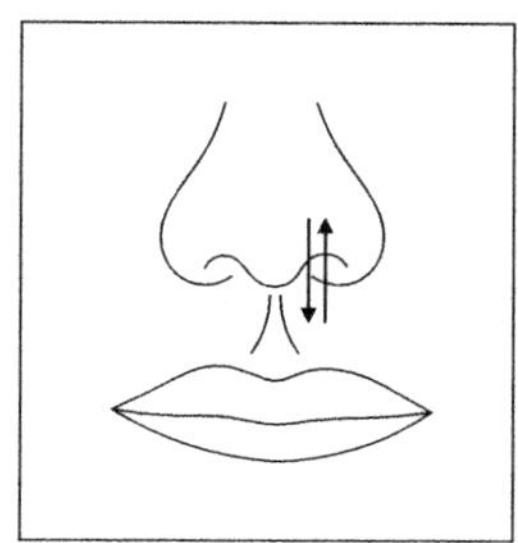

Do NOT visualize the flow of breath

Figure 6.2 **Shifting Flow of Breath – WRONG Technique**

Sushumna Kriya

Sushumna Kriya is an especially fine practice and when practiced daily over a long period of time, leads to dhyana. It should be practiced after Nadi Shodhanam without Vishnu Mudra.

Sit with the head, neck and trunk in a straight line. Sit in your chosen meditative posture with your eyes closed and do this practice silently.

Variation 1: Simple Sushumna Kriya

Allow your mind to focus at the crown of the head and gently exhale as though you are exhaling to the base of the spine. Inhale as though you are breathing from the base of the spine to the crown of the head without creating any disturbances in the breath flow (Fig. 6.3).

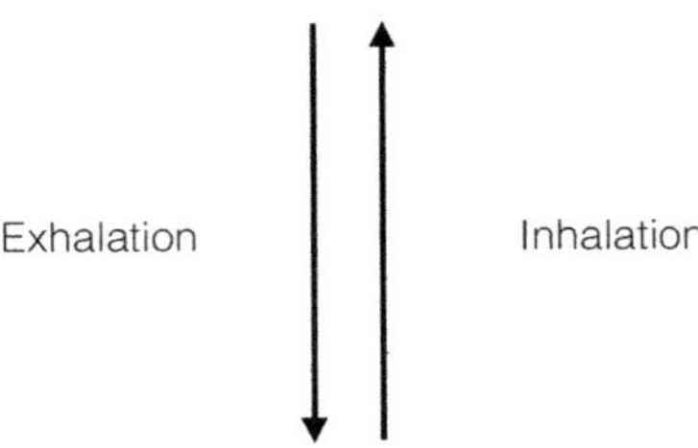

NOTE: Due to the limitations of the illustration this practice may be misunderstood. The illustration may give the impression that you exhale and inhale along the sides of the spine. This is not the case. Both exhalation and inhalation are along the central channel sushumna, that runs along the spine.

Figure 6.3 **Simple Sushumna Kriya**

Observe your mind and see how many times it becomes distracted. The moment the mind is distracted, you will find that there is a slight jerk or an irregularity in the breath. During this practice it is recommended that you continue the gentle flow of breath without jerks, noise, shallowness or extended pauses.

As your breath becomes smooth and silent, you may notice that there is still a slight pause after every inhalation and exhalation. To eliminate the pause entirely, you must learn to practice Variation 3, that is, Sushumna Kriya without Pause.

Variation 2: Sushumna Kriya with Soham

Having acquired some skill in practicing Simple Sushumna Kriya, you may introduce the mantra Soham. Exhale from the crown of the head as though you are exhaling to the base of the spine, listening to the sound "Ham" (Fig. 6.4). Inhale, as though you are breathing from the base of the spine to the crown of the head, listening to the sound "So."

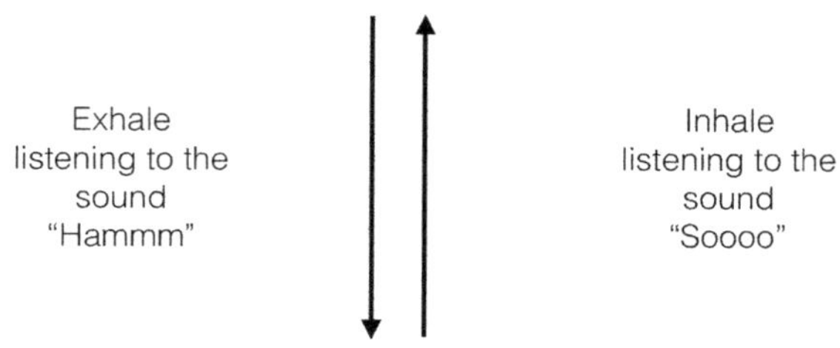

NOTE: Due to the limitations of the illustration this practice may be misunderstood. The illustration may give the impression that you exhale and inhale along the sides of the spine. This is not the case. Both exhalation and inhalation are along the central channel sushumna, that runs along the spine.

Figure 6.4 **Sushumna Kriya with Soham**

The choice of the words "listening to the sound" of the mantra is neither accidental nor an error. Listening is a passive sense of cognition; it is not an active sense organ like speech. Some teachers encourage the active repetition of the mantra as part of the Sushumna Kriya. While this may be useful for a short period of time, the practice of listening to the mantra is a finer practice. If you feel uncomfortable listening to Soham continue to do Simple Sushumna Kriya until the mantra Soham emerges naturally and effortlessly.

Variation 3: Sushumna Kriya without Pause

Even though you may have eliminated extended pauses, a slight pause causes a subtle but deep disturbance in the mind. When you remove even the slightest of pauses you gain deep insights into the mysteries of life and death. One who masters this practice is known as a pranavadin (Fig. 6.5).

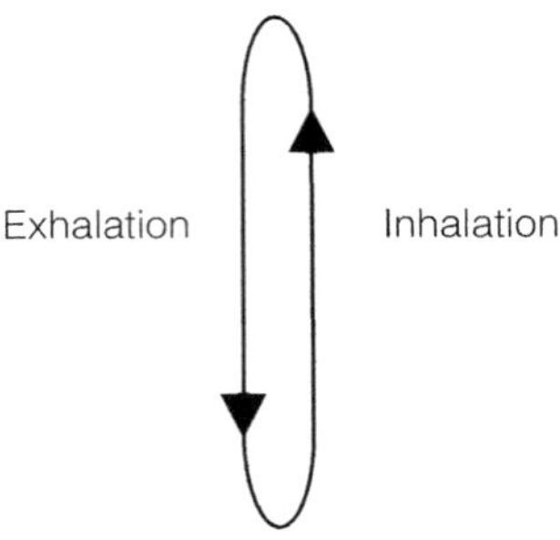

NOTE: Due to the limitations of the illustration this practice may be misunderstood. The illustration may give the impression that you exhale and inhale along the sides of the spine visualizing an oval form. This is not the case. This is not a visualization exercise and both exhalation and inhalation are along the central channel sushumna, that runs along the spine.

Figure 6.5 **Sushumna Kriya without Pause**

Sushumna Kriya without Pause is much finer than Simple Sushumna Kriya. You might notice something odd, when you practice Sushumna Kriya without Pause for a longer period of time: the many separate breathing exercises and pranayama practices seem to merge together and become one! This is a sign of great progress.

Practitioners often start visualizing an oval or a cylindrical tube as shown in the diagram. This is not a visualization practice. The diagram is only an aid to demonstrate that the exhalation flows into the inhalation and the inhalation flows into the exhalation. The mind moves along the spinal cord in sushumna and not along the sides of the spinal cord. Unless you master Sushumna Kriya without Pause, you will find it difficult to practice advanced pranayama, which eventually leads to Kumbhaka, the breathless state.

Variation 4: Sushumna Kriya with Aum

Having mastered Sushumna Kriya without Pause opens up the subtle and fine world of pranayama. You are ready for advanced practices that will lead to Kumbhaka. It only makes sense to practice Sushumna Kriya with Aum if you have mastered the practice of Sushumna Kriya without Pause and have already gained considerable insights into the mysteries of life and death. For millennia this fine and subtle practice was the sole privilege of pranavadins, who had devoted their entire lives to exploring this mystery.

TIP: The mantra Soham can be divided into two syllables, which are coordinated with the exhalation and inhalation. However, the mantra Aum is one syllable and cannot be divided. Therefore, it is an absolute prerequisite to master Variation 3, that is, Sushumna Kriya without Pause, before you practice Sushumna Kriya with Aum.

To practice Sushumna Kriya with Aum, allow the attention to travel from the crown of the head, as though you are exhaling to the base of the spine, listening to the sound "Aum." Inhale, as though you are breathing along the spine from the base of the spine to the crown of the head, listening to a deep and blissful silence (Fig. 6.6).

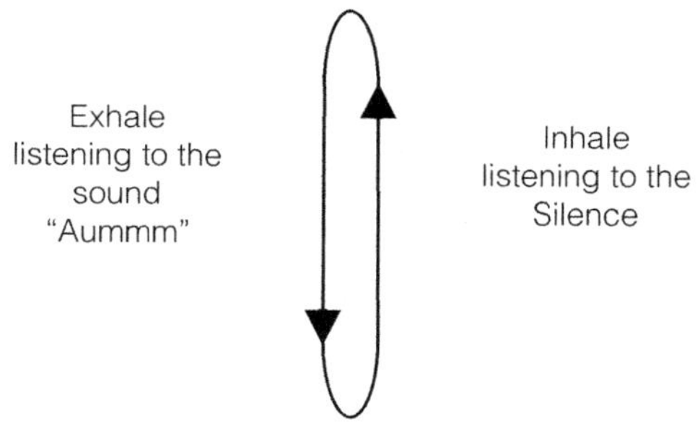

NOTE: Due to the limitations of the illustration this practice may be misunderstood. The illustration may give the impression that you exhale and inhale along the sides of the spine visualizing an oval form. This is not the case. This is not a visualization exercise and both exhalation and inhalation are along the central channel sushumna, that runs along the spine.

Figure 6.6 **Sushumna Kriya with Aum**

The Light of Sushumna

When you practice Sushumna Kriya correctly over a long and unbroken period of time, the sushumna channel opens and the light of sushumna emerges out of the darkness. This is not a mere visualization technique.

Some teachers and traditions practice Sushumna Kriya with visualization of the sushumna nadi. A far deeper and finer practice is to allow the light of sushumna nadi to emerge forward naturally and effortlessly. Creating artificial lights through a process of visualization prevents you from observing the far subtler universal light of sushumna within. This is only possible with long, uninterrupted systematic practice.

The Chakras

While practicing Sushumna Kriya, you may notice that the awareness travels along the spine through the energy points known as *chakras*. Most people have heard of *chakras*, though few know what they are and even fewer know, how to work with these. There are seven main *chakras* or energy points along the spine (Fig. 6.7). *Chakra* means "wheel."

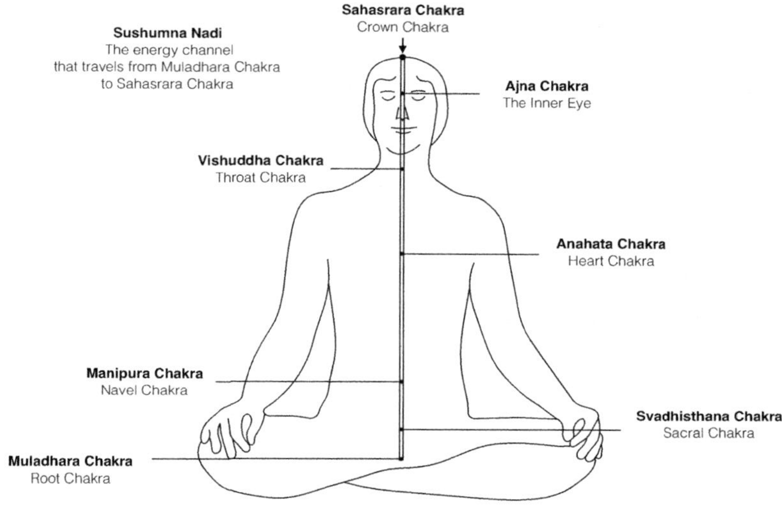

Figure 6.7 **Chakras and Sushumna Nadi**

Muladhara Chakra, the Root Chakra

This is the first chakra and it is located at the very base of the spine at the coccyx. It is related to the element earth. *Mula* means "root" and indicates that the person at this level has roots in the material and physical world in the form of attachments. Attachments keep us rooted with material and physical concerns. If your mind is pre-occupied with thoughts of material wealth and sensual pleasures, then you are unconsciously focusing on this chakra. Fear and self-preservation are the predominant aspects of this chakra.

All human beings have a tremendous potential. Most persons are unaware of this immense creative potential and only a small amount of this is tapped. This immense creative energy is called kundalini and it resides at the Muladhara Chakra.

Svadhisthana Chakra, the Sacral Chakra

Svadhisthana, the second chakra means "Her own abode." Though the kundalini energy resides at the Muladhara Chakra, this is her true abode.

The Svadhisthana Chakra is related to the element water. As you know, the human body, as well as our planet, comprises to a great extent of water. When this chakra is open, the creative energy begins to flow and the person becomes more aware and conscious.

Manipura Chakra, the Navel Chakra

This chakra is located at the solar plexus. The word *mani* means "gem" and *pura* means "city." This chakra, the city of gems, is the largest chakra. It regulates the digestive system and the flow of energy throughout the body. The element of this chakra is fire. The opening of this chakra releases many blockages in the energy flow throughout the body and brings with it greater health and well-being.

Anahata Chakra, the Heart Chakra

This chakra is located at the center of the chest, between the breasts. The Heart Chakra is related to the element air. While the Manipura Chakra is the powerhouse of energy, the Heart Chakra is the center of emotions.

The Heart Center is also the center of deep sleep, therefore meditation on this chakra can also make you drowsy. The upper and lower hemispheres of the body meet at this chakra. The Heart Chakra is the central chakra, with three chakras above and three below.

Vishuddha Chakra, the Throat Chakra

This chakra is located at the pit of the throat. It is related to the element of space. It is associated with creativity, arts, music and dance. Those, who are highly creative have unconsciously tapped the energy potential of this chakra.

Ajna Chakra, the Inner Eye

The first five chakras were associated with the five elements earth, water, fire, air and space. The sixth chakra, the Ajna Chakra goes beyond these elements; it is the seat of the mind. While worldly activities lie in the domain of the first five chakras, the Ajna Chakra is the gateway beyond the material world to the spiritual world.

The word Ajna is made up of two parts: the prefix *A* means "not" and *jna* is "knowledge." Thus, contrary to popular belief, this chakra is not the chakra of knowledge. The Ajna Chakra is one of the most difficult chakras to cross when leading the energy of kundalini to the Sahasrara Chakra or the Crown Chakra. Crossing the Ajna Chakra, the seat of the mind, means the practitioner has access to both, the conscious as well as the unconscious mind. It is beyond this chakra that the mysterious chakra of knowledge, known as the Guru Chakra, is located. Thus, the Ajna Chakra is the gatekeeper to the mystical higher chakras.

Sahasrara Chakra, the Crown Chakra

The last chakra is Sahasrara Chakra, the thousand petalled lotus. When the practitioner succeeds in raising the latent energy kundalini from the base of the spine, past the Ajna Chakra to this final chakra, he understands the mysteries of life and death, and rests in infinite joy and wisdom.

The Sahasrara Chakra is not associated with any elements, being beyond both mind as well as elements. It is the seat of Universal Consciousness and the acme of human aspirations.

Bhuta Shuddhi and Sushumna Kriya

Bhuta refers to the five elements of earth, water, fire, air and space. The *bhutas* have nothing to do with the actual elements. Earth is all that, which is stable and hard; it is smelt, tasted, seen and touched. Water is smooth; it is all that, which is tasted, seen and touched. Fire is all that, which is seen and touched. Air is all that, which is felt in space. Space is the medium in which these take place. Take, for instance, a juicy, red apple: The smell of the apple is the element earth. The juicy taste of the apple is the element of water. The color of the apple that you see is an aspect of fire. The smooth texture of the apple is felt due to air and the crunchy sound it makes, while you chew, is heard in space.

All your thoughts and mental images are made up of these elements. Thus, your memories are made up of these elements. The word *bhuta* also means "the past," and the word *shuddhi* means "purification." In this context, purification means letting go of the past and releasing this blocked energy.

Bhuta Shuddhi	Sushumna Kriya
Focuses awareness on different chakras along the spine	Allows the awareness to flow along the spine
Use of multiple mantras	Use of one mantra leading to silence
Practice of exhalation and inhalation without pause not possible	Practice of exhalation and inhalation without pause is trained
Lot of visualization required	No visualization required
Does not facilitate elongation of breath	Allows breath elongation
Does not lead to natural and effortless breath retention or Kumbhaka	Can lead to natural and effortless Kumbhaka
Encourages multi-pointedness	Promotes one-pointedness
Extremely complicated, done best with external guidance of teacher or recording	Simple to understand and practice, can be practiced independently without external aids

Table 6.1 **Comparison – Bhuta Shuddhi & Sushumna Kriya**

There has been a proliferation of techniques that go by the name of Bhuta Shuddhi. These different techniques of Bhuta Shuddhi are generally practiced in conjunction with visualization, mantra repetition and breath retention, which makes them extremely complicated. These practices require the practitioner to focus his awareness on the seven chakras from the Muladhara Chakra to the Sahasrara Chakra, one by one. The different versions of Bhuta Shuddhi encourage mantra repetition, counting and visualization. These are generally followed by the different variations of Nadi Shodhanam with breath retention and mantra repetition for a specific number of times. The practice of breath retention, counting and mantra repetition, together with change of nostril flow using Vishnu Mudra, takes you in the direction of multi-pointedness. Is it really possible for the awareness to be fine and subtle, and the mind to be still and internal, while attempting to juggle so many different activities?

Sushumna Kriya, on the other hand, is one of the finest versions of Bhuta Shuddhi and serves the purpose of purifying the body and mind, as well as releasing the blocked energy of past memories. Sushumna Kriya initiates and supports the process of Bhuta Shuddhi.

The various techniques of Bhuta Shuddhi are like a key instrument, such as a piano or an Indian harmonium. Sushumna Kriya, on the other hand, is similar to a string instrument, like a violin. Just as the violin can "flow" across the seven octaves to produce a very fine melody, the pranic energy flows through all the chakras in Sushumna Kriya without any obstacles.

Q&A

Question: When practicing Nadi Shodhanam without Vishnu Mudra, I get fidgety and restless. I jump up immediately, ending my practice session abruptly. Why does this happen and what can I do about it?

Answer: Shifting the nostril flow with the power of attention churns up the prana and helps to release negative energy. This may manifest at a physical level as uneasiness. You may unconsciously just jump out of your seat. To prevent this from happening, you must make sure that your posture is stable and the feet are interlocked. Interlocked feet make it a little more difficult to unconsciously jump out of a practice session. Having said this, there is no option other than to sit through the uneasiness: it will pass. It is possible to sit through this with determination.

Question: Can I combine any mantra with the breath instead of Soham or Aum?

Answer: Soham, a sound with two syllables is ideal to combine with the breath. It is a universal mantra and can be used by everyone. Aum, the one syllable sound, should only be combined with the breath after the practitioner has mastered breathing without pauses.

It is difficult to coordinate other mantras with the breath because they cause jerks and pauses in the breath. They also do not promote the equal breath. Using other mantras with the breath can disturb the prana and damage the pranic vehicles.

Question: Can I do Sushumna Kriya anytime in between when I have the time, instead of going through the entire sequence of practice?

Answer: Due to limitations of time, many practitioners use pranayama techniques anytime without going through the sequence that takes you from movement to stillness, from external to internal, from multi-pointedness to one-pointedness. This is not a systematic approach.

Those who have difficulties integrating the systematic approach in daily life, may take the shortcuts and do only a few techniques in their free time, but they should not expect speedy results. After doing unsystematic practice for years or even decades, practitioners wonder why they do not progress. To master pranayama and understand the mysteries of prana, you need uninterrupted, systematic practice over a long period of time.

Question: Why does one exhale from the Crown Chakra to the Root Chakra and then inhale and go up to Crown Chakra? I am more comfortable doing the opposite. I prefer to inhale and go to the Root Chakra and exhale and go up to the Crown Chakra. Can I continue to do it my way?

Answer: The natural tendency is to inhale and let the mind travel from the Crown Chakra to the Root Chakra. This is the natural flow of prana downward, just like the river flows down the mountain. If you want to return to the source of that infinite energy at the Crown Chakra then you have to go against the stream. This means you have to reverse the flow. You have to go against the natural tendency of inhaling and traveling down. Instead, you must inhale and travel upward. You have to go against the natural tendency of exhaling and letting the attention travel up to the Crown Chakra. Instead, you must exhale and letting the attention travel from the Crown Chakra to the Root Chakra.

This reversal may cause uneasiness and even a bit of confusion as your mind tries to wrestle with this strange, new, "reversed" way of breathing along the sushumna. After a while, this reversed way of breathing becomes the new natural. This may take a few days or even a few months. It all depends on how often you practice.

Continuing to do what you have been doing all along, will make this a simple breathing exercise. It is the reversal of prana and leading it upward that opens sushumna and makes this a pranayama practice.

Question: I find it difficult to do even the simple variation of Sushumna Kriya. The awareness seems to stop somewhere near at the Heart Chakra. I tried to bring up the awareness above the Heart Chakra but I find it difficult. Can you explain why this is happening and what I should do?

Answer: If you find it difficult to go beyond a certain chakra, it means that the chakra is blocked and the energy is not flowing freely. Everyone has blocks at one or the other chakra and it is not unusual to find that even the simple variation of Sushumna Kriya is difficult to practice.

If you are only able to do the practice until the Heart Chakra, then do the practice from the Root Chakra until the Heart Chakra and back. If you feel a block at the Vishuddha Chakra, the Throat Chakra and cannot go beyond, then keep doing the practice from the Root Chakra until the Throat Chakra and back. Doing this daily over a longer period of time will help release this block and eventually you will be able to do the practice up to the Crown Chakra.

Question: I have elongated the breath to approximately 20 counts each for exhalation and inhalation. I would like to practice Sushumna Kriya without Pause, however, I feel very uncomfortable and anxious when I try it. Why is this happening?

Answer: Most of us are so busy in the external world, we do not know how to go within. For some persons, even closing the eyes creates a sense of insecurity and vulnerability. This is why some people have difficulties with the practice.

When the breath has been elongated, you must drop the counts. As you train Sushumna Kriya without Pause, the mind withdraws inward and becomes contemplative. Your initial discomfort and anxiety indicates that the mind is, in fact, letting go of the external world and you are beginning to internalize. Do not stop at this stage. If you continue the practice, sushumna will open and blocked energy will be released in the form of repressed memories, fears and unfulfilled desires. This latent energy must be integrated gradually over a longer period of time.

Chapter 7

THE WEDDING OF THE SUN AND THE MOON

Twilight moments have kept mystics and poets busy since a long time, and not without reason. Twilight is that mystical moment when the mind is naturally contemplative. As you stand at the threshold of the inner world, the question you need to ask yourself is: "Do I really want to be an adept?"

If you have unlearned the faulty breathing habits, trained correct diaphragmatic breathing and systematically practiced the various breathing exercises over a long uninterrupted period of time, then you are ready to reap the benefits of deeper pranayama practices. After practicing and integrating Nadi Shodhanam and Sushumna Kriya in your daily life, you are ready to master one of the finest yogic practices: Sandhya Kriya.

Sandhya: The Meeting of Day and Night

Sandhya means "twilight." Dawn and dusk are the times of twilight, the transition from night to day and from day to night. Sandhya is a mystical time when day meets night and night meets day.

As you have already discovered, air flows through the nostrils activating ida and pingala alternately in a constant effort to maintain balance. The pranavadins experimented with the mind and breath over many generations and discovered that it was rare for both nostrils to flow freely. One of these rare moments was when the breath flow shifted from left to right and left again. This transition is so short lived that it is difficult to notice it. They sought to bring about this transition period consciously and to maintain it for longer periods of time. This is Sandhya Kriya. This simple yet subtle practice has many names. It is also known as Sushumna Awakening, Sushumna Application, Sukhamana or just Breath Awareness.

The technique of Sandhya is different from the meditative state known as Sandhya. The practice of Sandhya that leads to a natural meditative state is so simple that it is often underestimated and dismissed as "too simple." One of the most mystical practices, Sandhya leads to the threshold of the unconscious mind.

The Natural Cycles of our World

There are many cycles in nature: the cycle of day and night, the lunar cycle, the annual cycle of seasons and the shifting of the breath between the left and right nostrils. This change of flow is a natural cycle of the body like tides in the ocean. In a healthy person this process of nostril dominance will shift every 60–120 minutes. This is a physiological fact that was confirmed by the pranavadins thousands of years ago through empirical study. Having observed the breath cycle, the yogis continued their experiments and discovered the connection between the breath and the mind. They concluded:

- When the left nostril flows freely, the feminine qualities are active.
- When the right nostril flows freely, the masculine qualities are active.

The human body is made of two currents, feminine and masculine, known as ida and pingala respectively. You are subject to the shifting flow of these dualities constantly, like the tides that ebb and flood. The moon and the sun are symbols of the dualities; of day and night, man and woman, black and white, happiness and sadness, hot and cold, right and left, up and down. When the wedding of the sun and moon takes place, then one goes beyond all dualities.

On carrying out their experiments, the pranavadins discovered that when the breath flows occasionally through both nostrils simultaneously, the mind attains a state of joy, known as *sukhamana*, "the joyous mind." The mind goes naturally inward and travels to deeper levels of consciousness. The mind experiences intense joy in this state of balance.

How to practice Sandhya Kriya

Even after practicing Nadi Shodhanam and Sushumna Kriya one nostril may be more dominant. This means you need to consciously open the passive nostril without blocking the dominant or active nostril. This is also called Sushumna Application. There are four methods to practice Sushumna Application.

With external aids

1. applying pressure under the arms
2. lying on the opposite side
3. with Vishnu Mudra

Method 1 and Method 2 are not recommended, being unsuitable for advanced pranayama and dhyana. Method 3 is acceptable, though only as a transition to Method 4.

Without external aids

4. using attention or awareness

The finest method is the fourth, without Vishnu Mudra or any sort of external aids.

Method 3: With Vishnu Mudra

Check, which nostril is flowing freely and which one is blocked by holding the forefinger before the nostrils. Use Vishnu Mudra to close the nostril that is already flowing freely. This will force the flow of breath through the nostril that is blocked.

The disadvantage of this technique is that the dominant nostril must be closed. This may cause subtle disturbances in the flow of prana. This technique could also cause the dominant nostril to be blocked, thus, once again, leaving us with only one nostril flowing freely. Another disadvantage of this method is that it brings you back to the level of the body.

Method 4: Without Vishnu Mudra

Sandhya Kriya is a simple technique of paying attention. Close your eyes and let your mind rest at the space between the two nostrils (Fig. 7.1). Observe the flow of air between both the nostrils in the mind‘s eye. If both nostrils are flowing freely you are practicing Sandhya.

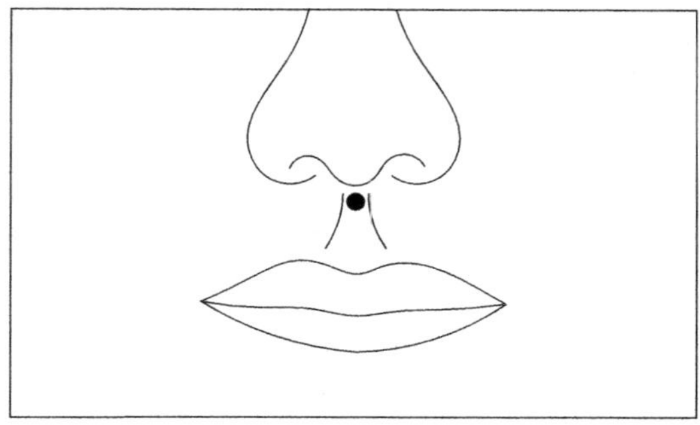

Pay attention to the space between the nostrils called Nasagre

Figure 7.1 **Sandhya – RIGHT Technique**

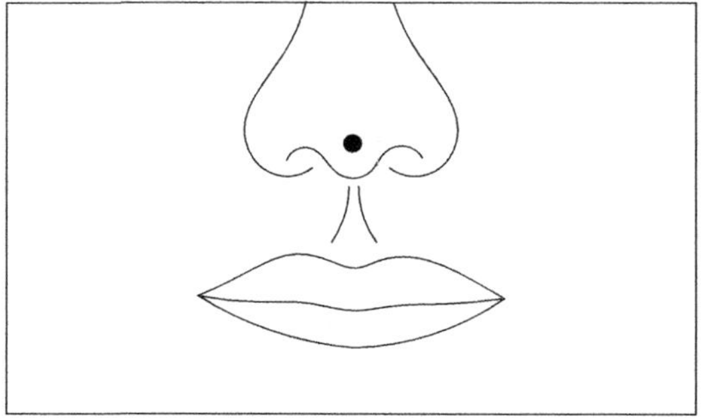

NOT tip of the nose or any other point

Figure 7.2 **Sandhya – WRONG Technique**

There are many misunderstandings about where exactly the attention should rest. Yoga literature uses the term *Nasagre*. This is often mistaken to mean the tip of the nose (Fig. 7.2). This is incorrect. Concentration at the tip of the nose is another exercise, known as Trataka. Since you cannot feel the breath at the tip of the nose, you cannot balance ida and pingala there. *Nasagre* is the spot between both the nostrils (Fig. 7.1). *Nasas* are "nostrils."

If you have been practicing systematically, then you will feel the subtle flow of breath at Nasagre, even without testing it with your forefinger. If you have been practicing Nadi Shodhanam and Sushumna Kriya daily, over a long period of time, you may notice that both the nostrils are open. If you observe that only one nostril is flowing freely after Nadi Shodhanam and Sushumna Kriya, then allow your attention to rest at the space before the blocked nostril. Use awareness and will power to open the closed nostril and you will be surprised to notice that in a few seconds time the blocked nostril has opened. If you have mastered the technique of Nadi Shodhanam, especially Variation 3, this should not be difficult. While it may sound incredible to use the power of attention to get the nostril to flow freely, if you have prepared yourself and practiced systematically, this is possible. This leads to Sandhya, the wedding of the sun and the moon. A sure sign of Sandhya is intense, reasonless joy. The joy is so intense, it seems the heart will burst! The other clear sign is that both nostrils start flowing freely.

Sukhamana: Threshold to an Unknown World

Attempting to skip the correction of faulty breathing patterns, or dropping practices, such as Nadi Shodhanam and Sushumna Kriya, to go directly to Sandhya is a waste of time. If you do not go about this systematically, you are bound to fail and this will result in frustration.

It is only when both nostrils are freely flowing that sushumna, the central channel, is open. When you learn how to wed the sun and the moon, the mind becomes joyous. You prepare to awaken kundalini by understanding the relationship between the right breath and the left breath and learning to apply Sandhya, the wedding of the sun and the moon.

Inviting the Hidden to come forward

When sushumna is open, you are at the threshold of the unconscious mind. A well prepared student, who is fearless, invites the hidden to come forward. For beginners of dhyana this means you are coming in touch with the first layer of unacceptable qualities.

The unacceptable qualities are the many layers of thoughts, feelings and memories, which the conscious mind does not wish to be identified with. As the meditator progresses in the internal journey, he comes in touch with the deepest recesses of the mind, including:

1. Memories and Emotions: Memories are not acceptable when they are too painful and unpleasant. Besides these unacceptable memories, there are also emotions that are perceived as unacceptable, such as anger and jealousy.
2. Fears: Some fears are universal, such as that of poverty, loneliness, disease, old age, and death. Other fears are more individual in nature, such as fear of spiders, snakes, heights, darkness or closed spaces.
3. Desires: Many desires are unacknowledged and remain unfulfilled such as desires for material possessions, fame and success. The strong sexual desire and the primitive urge for offspring also dominate our lives.

It is not possible to bypass the difficult and dangerous terrain of the unconscious mind on the internal journey. This is why guidance on the internal journey is absolutely necessary, until the meditator is experienced enough. Those rare few, who know their way in the dark forest of the unconscious mind, have access to the immense and limitless potentials. These rare masters know the secret of the three worlds: the three states of waking, dreaming and deep sleep. These seers and sages speak a mystical language known as Sandhya *Bhasha*, the "twilight language."

Sandhya Bhasha: Mystical Language of the Sages

Bhasha means "language." Though scholars have translated Sandhya Bhasha as the twilight language, it is not really a language. Sandhya Bhasha can be used only for the communication of mystical matters. It is a language of symbols and contains no vocabulary for the matters of the world. For instance, Sandhya, the transition period, when the day weds the night is not merely a period of time caused by the rotation of the earth. It has many layers of meanings.

Sandhya is:

1. a simple technique to allow the breath to flow freely from both nostrils.
2. a simple form of meditation, allowing the mind to be aware of the breath at the meeting of both open nostrils, letting the thoughts rise and drop away.
3. the mystical threshold to the unconscious state of mind, where the practitioner gains access to the immense potentials of the mind and learns Sandhya Bhasha, the twilight language spoken only by yogis.
4. the transition to the other shore, where all mysteries of life and death are revealed.

The one who knows the secret of the three states of consciousness has access to the immense potentials of the unknown and the meaning of different symbols are revealed to him. Such a one has access to the library of infinite wisdom and knowledge. The most ancient of all mysteries, the mystery of death and life is unveiled before him, since Sandhya is also the transition between death and life and death again. To such a one all questions fall away, and the Truth reveals itself. Nothing remains to be done. All is a play of consciousness. Such a one is master of the Self and knows how to live in the world, yet above it.

Q&A

Question: How long does it take to master Sushumna Application or Sandhya with mental focus, that is, without use of Vishnu Mudra?

Answer: This really depends on how often you practice. If you practice daily with determination you could master Sandhya Kriya within a couple of months. If you are irregular in your practice, it may take years. Generally, those who are irregular in practice, get frustrated and go back to using Vishnu Mudra; they never master Sandhya.

Experience has shown that if the preparation is systematic, then with daily practice, it is possible for a good student to master Sushumna Application without Vishnu Mudra, using only will power, in just ten days.

Chapter 8

HOLDING ON TO THE THREAD OF AWARENESS

Life is a wondrous rainbow. As you transition from one color to another, you discover, there are no compartments, no divisions; just beautiful shades that flow into each other. Awareness is the thread that takes you through the transitions of life as well as death.

The repeated shifts of air flow between the two nostrils and the changing states of the mind are natural and continuous. When the pranavadins discovered these rhythms, they wanted to go beyond the dualities of the sun and the moon by opening sushumna. They studied and experimented with the breath, the mind and prana itself to develop the science of pranayama.

Principles of Advanced Pranayama

An important aspect of the 7 Step Program is to understand the three main principles of this ancient science:

Movement to stillness

If you observe yourself carefully during practice, you notice that the body is constantly moving and it is difficult to sit still. The mind is also moving and you have a hard time focusing on one subject for a longer period of time. Through systematic practice, you train a continuously moving body to sit still for longer, let your mind calm down and focus your attention on a single subtle, internal object. It is not possible to just sit down and forcefully calm oneself. Even if you would succeed in doing that, a strong undercurrent of tension would disturb you at an unconscious level.

External to internal

The external world is a busy place and a huge amount of impressions and stimuli are taken in by the cognitive senses: sight, hearing, taste, smell and touch. The information is processed in the mind and communicated to the external world through the active senses such as speech. This keeps the mind busy in the external world.

One important aspect of the systematic approach is the training of the senses. The practitioner seeks to shift the focus from the active senses to cognitive senses, for instance, from talking to listening. According to yogic literature, there are five active as well as five cognitive senses. While we are all familiar with the cognitive senses from modern science, we do not know the active senses. The active senses are: speech, grasping, locomotion, reproduction and excretion. In these five activities the mind is oriented outward. It is important to remember the terminology used in the ancient sciences cannot always be accurately translated since there are no parallels in the modern sciences. Locomotion, for instance, is not just movement of the body using the legs. If you wave goodbye, smile or even just glance at someone, there is a movement with which you communicate with the external world. In fact, most of our communication is unconscious and expressed unconsciously through body language. It is hard to imagine saying goodbye without moving any single part of the body.

In a systematic practice you go from the external world to the body, to the breath and become aware of your conscious mind and eventually start to explore the unconscious mind. As sushumna opens, you go from the gross world of objects to the subtler realm of internal objects in thoughts and memories.

Multi-pointedness to one-pointedness

With systematic practice you learn how to make the mind one-pointed. One of the main aspects is organizing your external environment. When the mind is constantly trained to jump from one activity to another or from one object to another, it is not possible to have a one-pointed mind.

An essential precondition is that all the three criteria mentioned above are met and not only one. It is possible for your attention to be internally focused, but your mind may be constantly moving from one thought to another. It is possible that you are physically still, but your mind is thinking about the external world.

The Margas: The Three Paths

The study of the *margas* is an important aspect of the science of pranayama. *Marga* means "path." Awareness takes three paths. These were studied and well-documented by the pranavadins. To master pranayama the practitioner must observe and analyze all the three paths.

Dissolution

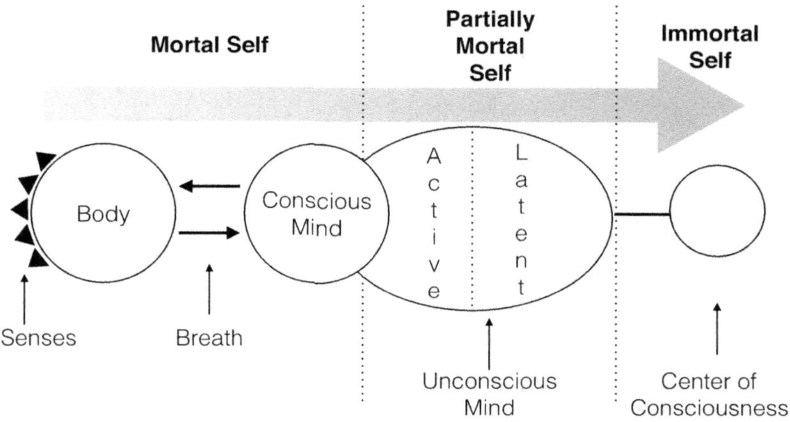

Figure 8.1 **Nivritti Marga – Dissolution**

Nivritti Marga is when the awareness turns inward from the external world to the body, moving towards the mind and eventually to the source of all prana (Fig. 8.1). *Nivritti* means "cessation," "returning," or "dissolution." This internal journey leads away from the many worldly objects towards spiritual attainments.

Manifestation

The shifting of the awareness from the subtle-most towards the body and the worldly objects is known as *Pravritti* Marga (Fig. 8.2). *Pravritti* means "coming forth" or "manifestation."

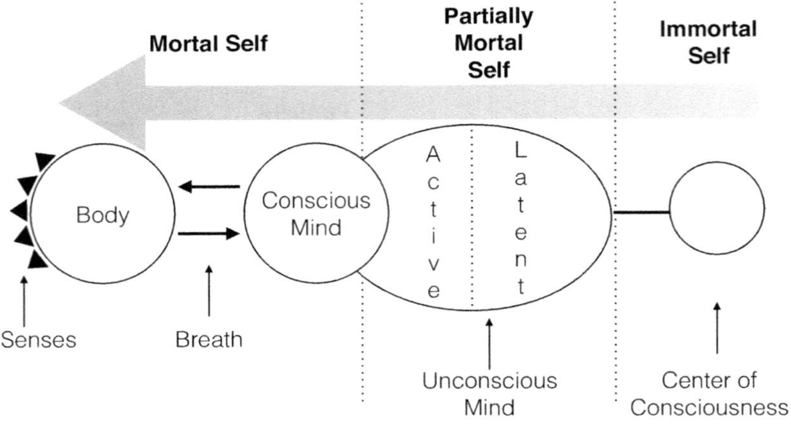

Figure 8.2 **Pravritti Marga – Manifestation**

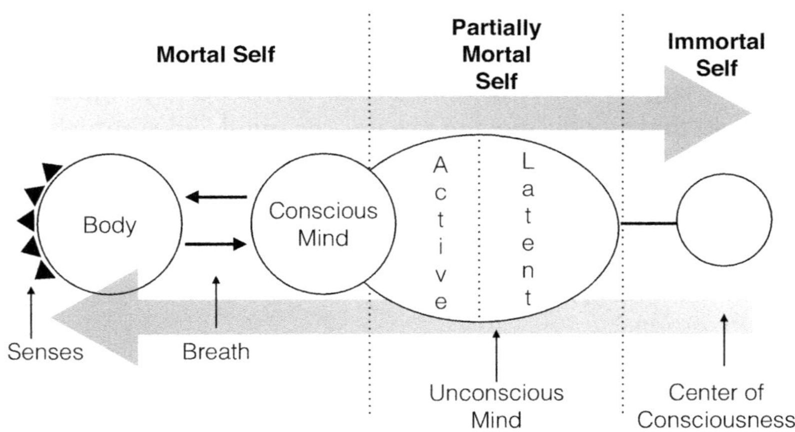

Figure 8.3 **Purna Marga – Complete Path**

The Complete Path

The laws of the internal and the external world are different.

When we understand these laws and live in harmony with both, then we are masters of both, the internal and external paths. This is called *Purna* Marga (Fig. 8.3). *Purna* means "complete."

The Transitions

When you first looked at the yogic anatomy (Fig. 1.1) in Chapter 1, you saw separate parts; there was the mortal self, the semi-mortal self and the immortal Self. You also saw parts such as body, breath, mind and Pure Consciousness. We tend to think that the body is separate from the breath and mind, that these are all separate entities. When you understand the subtleties of the breath, you realize that the body, breath, mind and Pure Consciousness are not compartmentalized, in fact, they are intricately interwoven. When you train the senses to turn inward and observe the body and the breath, you start becoming more aware of the conscious mind and sushumna opens. As you continue to explore, you may unlock the potential of the active unconscious mind and eventually the latent unconscious mind as well. This takes you finally to Adi Prana and the Center of Consciousness itself. When you realize this flow leads to the Center of Consciousness, which in turn permeates the universe, then you know that all this is part of one continuum. There are no compartments, no divisions; just beautiful shades that flow into each other.

Guiding Principle

Keeping the example of the caterpillar and the leaves in mind, the sages observed that the caterpillar does not jump from one leaf to another. It moves slowly and gradually and at one point the caterpillar is on both leaves. This is the transition.

Mastering pranayama means mastering the transition from movement to stillness; from external to internal; from multi-pointedness to one-pointedness. This transition from the gross to the subtle does not happen instantly or in an abrupt manner; it is smooth and gentle. For instance, when you go a bit deeper into the breathing practices, you may hear the sound of the breath singing Soham; this is a transition from actively regulating your breath to listening to the sound of the mantra.

The Fourth Pranayama is Prana itself

As you master the process of awareness going gradually from gross to subtle, you will notice many different transitions that are regulated in four ways:

1. Space: Space is one aspect of the regulation of prana. At the most gross level, it is regulated through the awareness of the breath that is located physically at the diaphragm in diaphragmatic breathing or at the nostrils during Nadi Shodhanam. As the pranayama becomes more subtle, it is regulated internally along the spine as in Sushumna Kriya or along the different parts of the body in the various practices of Shavyatra, Shitalikarana and Yoga Nidra that you will learn in Chapter 11 of this book.

2. Time: The length of exhalation and inhalation can be regulated to make it equal and balanced through the different variations of Sushumna Kriya and other practices such as Aum Kriya. This is the second aspect to be considered in the process of mastering pranayama.

3. Count: The length of exhalation and inhalation can be made longer (*Dirgha*) and finer (*Suksma*). This is the third and a very important aspect to be considered in the process of mastering pranayama. It can be mastered through the different variations of Sushumna Kriya and various other pranayama practices such as Aum Kriya.

4. The Fourth: There is still another aspect of pranayama to be considered: it is known simply as the Fourth. The fourth pranayama is very mysterious: it is prana itself. On understanding the principles of advanced pranayama practices, you see the importance of progression from gross to subtle, to the subtle-most. At the subtle-most level, we have prana itself, also known as Adi Prana. It is through the practice and mastery of the fourth pranayama that the veil covering the light of Pure Consciousness is thinned and eventually destroyed.

Why is it that most of us are not experiencing the fourth pranayama? Why do some practitioners not attain even after decades of what they call practice? There are various reasons.

Nine Factors influencing your Practice

There are nine factors that constantly influence your progress in mastering Pranayama.

1. Adhikara: The first and foremost reason is talent. Some people are talented at art and others are terrible at it. Others are natural dancers and then there are those, who seem to be born with two left legs. The same applies to progress on the internal journey.

Adhikara means "authority" or "qualification." A naturally qualified student is known as an *adhikari.*

2. Method: Even if you are not an adhikari, you can experience the fourth pranayama through the right method and effort. There are three kinds of methods: Mild, medium and speedy. If you have a method that is very effective, you may get some glimpses of Pure Consciousness and with effort over a period of time eventually be established in it. The most speedy and effective method is one that takes you directly from gross to the subtle and eventually to the subtle-most.

3. Guidance: There are teachers training courses in which you can become a teacher in two hundred hours stretched over a year or two. There are also 600-hour teachers training courses. However,

it is known that you need around 10,000 hours of training in any particular field to attain mastery in it.

The Oral Tradition is an unbroken lineage from teacher to student; it is over 6,000 years old. It has already done the experimentation, so you do not need to experiment. A good teacher from an authentic tradition will provide you with guidance that is priceless. You do not need to experiment, instead you take the most speedy and direct path, the one that has proven itself to be the highway.

4. Consistency of Practice: Having a teacher and an efficient method from an authentic Tradition is an essential prerequisite but you also need consistency. One of the most common reasons that students do not progress, in spite of having all the above, is that they do not stay with one teacher, one method and one Tradition. Jumping from one teacher to another, even within a Tradition, causes setbacks. Changing your method of practice or constantly shopping for new practices disturbs the student and creates obstacles.

5. Uninterrupted Practice over a Long Period of Time: Erratic practice causes dissipation of energy. It is important to focus one's energy and keep doing the same practice daily over a long period of time. For speedy progress, practice four times a day. This is only for those with a burning desire for attainment and a sense of urgency. If you do not feel a sense of urgency, then two times or even once a day will suffice.

6. Preparation: Very often, students skip the preparation. Everybody wants to be advanced, but you do not become advanced by just skipping the basics.

7. Suitable Environment: Creating a suitable environment is important. One important aspect is having privacy or a bit of solitude. Solitude does not mean that you need to retire from your job or go to a silent retreat somewhere. It also does not mean that you have to give up family and friends and isolate yourself. All it means is that you need a small, airy room in your house. If you do not have a spare room, you can re-arrange the furniture to create a corner in a part of your house that is not very busy.

Creating a suitable environment also means organizing your life around your practice time. You need to have an agreement with your family; explain to them that this is important for you and demonstrate with concrete actions that you will not neglect your duties to the family.

One important factor in creating a suitable environment is beyond our control: the quality of air. During certain practices like Kapalabhati and Bhastrika the intake of air increases. If the air is extremely polluted, it may compound the ill-effects of polluted air. It is a serious disadvantage if you are living in an extremely polluted environment. You would have to discuss this with your teacher and find suitable alternatives to those few practices.

8. Satsang: *Sat* means "truth." *Sangha* is "the gathering." Thus, *satsang* is "gathering together in the name of truth." If you keep the company of thieves, sooner or later, the police is going to come knocking at your door, even if you have not stolen anything. It is important that you keep the right company; that is what satsang is about. It is not easy to keep the balance between solitude and company: either we get into excessive company or we end up isolating ourselves. If we are too external, we dissipate our energy; if we get isolated, we end up feeling lonely and dull. If you are very externally oriented, you will keep putting a lot of new impressions in your mind. When you sit down to practice, all these impressions will come up and disturb you. If you want to go deeper on the internal journey, you need to make certain life choices and changes in your lifestyle. Though an excessive lifestyle can be counter-productive, this does not mean that you need to isolate yourself. You need to promote a stable and quiet life with well selected companions. Mere practice without change in lifestyle will show only limited results. One way to maintain this balance is by keeping the right company. An important aspect of satsang is associating with the teacher who guides you.

9. Lifestyle or Regulation of Primitive Urges: The four primitive urges are sex, food, sleep and self-preservation. We cannot really

control these primitive urges, but we can try to find a healthy balance without excessive indulgence or strict repression. Since the four primitive urges are very important the entire next chapter is devoted to it.

Q&A

Question: I am a busy person and do not have the time to do a long and systematic practice. Can I skip all the different breathing exercises and go directly to advanced pranayama practices?

Answer: This question has been asked by many generations of students before and the Oral Tradition gives a beautiful response: Go out on a clear, moonless night and look for the North Star.

The North Star is fixed in the same position and for hundreds of years sailors and travelers have oriented themselves with the help of this star. However, you will discover that it is not easy to find the North Star since it is small and not very bright. To find the North Star, one must first find the bright star constellation called the Big Dipper. Once you found this constellation, it is easy to find the North Star.

The grosser breathing exercises are like the Big Dipper and the finer and deeper pranayama practices are like the North Star. While you may be able to go through the motions of advanced practices, it is highly unlikely that you will reach any depth in pranayama practice without going through the breathing exercises.

Chapter 9

THE IMPORTANCE OF LIFESTYLE OR HOW TO ENJOY LIFE

Life has so much to offer, but there is such a thing as "too much of a good thing." Do not be afraid of discipline. Discipline is your friend. Enjoy life with complete awareness and you will soon notice that even the coffee tastes much better.

While it is useful to learn and practice different breathing exercises and pranayama practices, you need to understand how primitive urges impact your lifestyle as well as your progress in pranayama. The primitive urges must be skillfully regulated so that the pranic energy is not dissipated. Instead, the pranic energy is channelized to bring happiness and success into every aspect of your life.

The four primitive urges are:

- Sexuality
- Food
- Sleep
- Self-Preservation

Sexuality

Regulating sexuality does not mean you have to lead a life of celibacy. A promiscuous lifestyle, on the other hand, can be just as harmful as repressed sexuality. Both excessive indulgence as well as suppression can cause disturbances in the pranic vehicles. Having a deeper relationship based on mutual respect with a partner goes a long way toward maintaining physical as well as mental health.

Food and sleep are grosser aspects of the primitive urges, since they are required for the immediate maintenance of the body. However, on further contemplation, you may realize that the sexual urge is deeply connected to the most powerful of all primitive urges: self-preservation. The sexual urge has been deeply ingrained in us, so that we have offsprings and ensure that humanity does not die out. The sexual urge manifests most strongly when the body is mature, healthy and capable of child bearing and child raising. The desire for sexual union is an external manifestation of the natural desire within us to merge with the eternal.

The sexual urge has been highly distorted and is associated with great shame, secrecy and taboo. This is why it is important to see it as just another appetite. Just as we experience hunger for food, we also experience a sexual appetite. If we can regulate our food habits through regular intake of meals, why do we find it strange to do the same for the sexual appetite? Sexuality, too, can be satisfied on a regular basis, such as 2–4 times a week, with a steady partner. Both partners are then mentally as well as physically prepared, taking the time to enjoy each other's company. In this way, sexuality can be transformed from a physical need to respectful and considerate companionship.

Here are some important points to remember:

- Regulate sexuality with a single, intimate partner.
- Promote a healthy relationship with your partner based on mutual respect and participation in each other's lives.
- Maintain regular days and times for sexual union with your partner. This prepares you physically and mentally.

Food

What we eat has a tremendous effect on our practice. Anything that is not water, is considered to be food. There are three kinds of foods: sattvic, rajasic and tamasic. When we speak about diet here, we are talking about diet with respect to yogic practice. Foods that are light and easy to digest are sattvic. Sattvic foods promote and support yogic practice. Rajasic and tamasic foods should be avoided.

Tamasic foods make the body feel heavy and the mind dull. They include frozen foods and processed foods. Foods with artificial coloring, aromas and preservatives are also tamasic. Food that is overcooked, reheated too often, deep fried or kept overnight is considered to be tamasic. Mushrooms and aged cheese are also tamasic. Breads with yeast are tamasic, therefore flatbreads are to be preferred. Red meats, such as beef, lamb and pork are also tamasic. White sugar, all sugary drinks and aerated drinks are tamasic too. Alcohol, drugs and all kinds of intoxicants fall into this category.

Rajasic foods stimulate the mind and body. In excess, they cause irritation, aggression, hyperactivity and sleeplessness. Extremely pungent food is rajasic. Heavy grains like wheat and heavy lentils are also rajasic. Garlic, chillies, and onions, are rajasic as well. Hot beverages such as black tea, green tea and coffee are rajasic. White meats, such as poultry and fish are rajasic. Eggs too, are rajasic.

Sattvic foods are those that purify the body and do not allow toxins to build up in the body. They are freshly cooked and easy to digest. Almost all fruit and vegetables are sattvic; figs and lemons are especially sattvic. Grains like unpolished rice and oats are sattvic. Buckwheat and millet are also considered to be sattvic. Legumes, such as mung dal, chickpeas, chana dal as well as mung beans are sattvic. Spices, such as fresh ginger, turmeric, coriander, cumin, cardamon, cinnamon and saffron are sattvic. Among milk products, fresh yogurt and ghee are sattvic. Sweeteners like natural honey and jaggery are sattvic. Seeds like sesame and flax are sattvic. Sprouts of different varieties also fall into this category.

A sattvic diet is one with a lot of variety and color. Foods of different color provide us with all the nutrition we require, such as green spinach, purple blueberries, orange papayas, red beetroots and yellow mangoes.

Milk was considered to be sattvic, but these days the milk is tamasic due to the industrial processes of homogenization, pasteurization, etc. The huge dairies with poor air, light and space conditions cause stress for the cows. Under these conditions the cows cannot give sattvic milk. Organic milk is an option to consider, since the cows live in better conditions. Another option to consider is goat's milk or sheep's milk since these are not as industrialized as cow's milk.

Among fats and oils, sesame oil and ghee are sattvic. Always use filtered oils, also called Native or Native Virgin oil. Do not use refined and processed oils. Processed and refined oils fall into the category of tamasic foods.

Use rock salt; it contains different trace elements and minerals. Never use refined salt. Refined salt falls into the category of tamasic foods.

Always practice before meals since it is not possible to practice on a full stomach. If you are doing four practices a day, do a morning practice before breakfast, midday practice before lunch, evening practice before a light and early evening meal and then a fourth practice before going to bed at night. If you want to practice after a meal, you need to wait for two hours after a light meal or four hours after a heavy meal.

The best kind of fast is the daily fast. The word breakfast comes from "break the fast." Every night you fast and this daily fast should ideally be around 12–14 hours long. If you finish dinner at around 8 p.m., you can eat breakfast after 8 a.m. next morning. This gives the body the entire night not only to digest the food but also enough time for deeper cleansing and regeneration. The daily fast is one of the best things that you can do for your overall well-being. If you eat a heavy meal, it is best to keep a fourteen hour fast. Crash diets and extreme fasts are not necessary as long as you keep the daily 12–14 hour fast. The daily fast is suitable for healthy persons. Those who have any health issues should consult a physician before trying the daily fast.

Eat slowly and with awareness. To increase your awareness while eating, it might be useful to count the number of times you chew your food. Absent-minded eating of food while walking, watching television, surfing the internet, reading books or comics is not healthy. This can lead to overeating, eventually to obesity, diabetes and other health issues. Never overeat. The yogis have a hand rule for food intake: fill half the stomach with solids, quarter with liquids (not water) and keep a quarter empty.

As far as possible eat freshly cooked and mildly spiced foods. Avoid heavy foods, especially in the evening. Have regular meals at fixed times; this prepares the body and mind for the absorption and assimilation of food. Those who are busy and travel a lot, need to find flexible and creative solutions, such as carrying healthy home cooked meals.

Drink around two liters of liquids through the day. This quantity is only a rough indication. You may need more liquids when down with fever or diarrhea, after sports, in summer or after exposure to cold air. Avoid sugary drinks like aerated drinks. Make yourself herbal tea instead of tea and coffee. Pour hot water over fresh ginger and your ginger tea is ready. You can do the same with peppermint leaves or tulsi leaves. You can also make a delicious herbal mix with different spices such as saffron, cardamom, cloves and cinnamon.

You can experiment a bit to see how food impacts you. Most of the time you will notice that food is deeply connected with emotions. When sad or disappointed you want to eat comfort foods like chocolate. Food is not just for the nourishment of the body. You need to observe how food affects the mind and nourishes it. Most of us are motivated by our sense of taste rather than the appetite. Often we experience a hunger for food that is determined by the taste and memories. As far as possible, eat only when really hungry; do not burden the stomach with more food, if there is no appetite.

Some important points to remember:

- Drink 1–2 liters of water everyday.
- Keep a daily 12–14 hour fast at night.
- Fill half the stomach with food, one quarter with liquids other than water and keep one quarter empty. Never overeat.
- Do not eat between meals. Have 3–4 meals daily at regular times.
- Do not keep food overnight. Prepare food daily.
- Eat slowly and consciously.
- Avoid coffee, black and green tea. Drink freshly made herbal teas without sugar instead.
- Eat only when you are hungry.

Sleep

Since we cannot interfere too much with the natural sleep patterns, regulating this primitive urge is all the more difficult.

There are many misguided practitioners who believe that once they practice some sort of asanas or do a little of what they call meditation, they do not need sleep at all or need just a couple of hours of sleep. Some drink coffee and energy drinks to stave off sleep. Extreme disturbance of the sleep pattern can cause serious damage to mental and physical health. Interference with the sleep pattern is dangerous.

Good quality sleep means no disturbance during sleep. A sick person generally does not have good quality sleep. Emotional disturbance also means poor quality sleep. Noise and light pollution also cause disturbances in sleep. Most of us need around 2–3 hours of deep sleep and 5–6 hours of dream time. Sleep deficiency leads to poor concentration, depression and anxiety, loss of memory and impaired learning ability. It also accelerates aging, impairs judgment and causes accidents. Sleep deprivation has also been connected to increase in appetite, eventually resulting in obesity.

It has also been observed that excessive food causes dullness, drowsiness and inevitably sleepiness. Thus, it is clear that the four primitive urges are deeply connected to each other and influence each other.

These days, it is difficult to maintain regular sleep patterns due to the strong influence of mobile technology and other media such as internet and television in our daily lives. Most people leading modern lifestyles work long hours and get too little sleep. They build up a huge sleep deficit and try to compensate on weekends. This leads to irregular sleeping patterns causing mood swings between hyperactivity and sloth. Getting a healthy amount of sleep is important. For most people 7–8 hours of good quality sleep is sufficient, except in the case of infants, adolescents, the sick, and pregnant women. These generally need more sleep. If you sleep too long, you might feel heavy, dull and experience sloth. If you sleep too little, you may get irritable, impatient and snappy. As one gets older, one needs less sleep. Those above the age of forty years may find themselves sleeping less or sleeping lightly.

Daytime naps or power naps are useful, especially for those who work a lot and are extremely stressed. If it is possible, lie down for 15–20 minutes. This will rest your body and mind. Do not fall asleep. The short rest will make you more creative and fresh for the rest of the day. Do not nap for longer than twenty minutes.

It may not be easy, but it is important, to work out a good bedtime ritual that helps you wind down. Go to bed at the same time every evening and wake up at the same time every morning. Most people use the time before bedtime for watching television and surfing the internet. The continuous movement of images disturbs the mind instead of soothing it. It is best not to watch television and surf the internet at least an hour before bedtime. It is also recommended that you put your mobile phone on airplane mode, at least an hour before bedtime. Turn off all devices and even better, do not keep any devices, such as mobiles and laptops, in your bedroom. Choose a bedtime ritual that soothes the mind, for instance, enjoy a relaxed stroll, practice meditation or read a page from a book that calms the mind and strengthens positive thoughts.

Avoid drinking coffee, black tea and green tea after 2 p.m. since these disturb the sleeping patterns. You can drink herbal teas, a warm fresh lemon drink with honey or just hot water instead. Do not eat a heavy dinner or indulge in after-dinner snacking in the evening.

Here are some points to remember:

- Go to bed at the same time every day.
- Wake up at the same time every day.
- Get around 7–8 hours of quality sleep.
- Have a dark and quiet room as your bedroom. Air out the room regularly.
- Avoid keeping devices in your bedroom.
- Do not drink coffee, black tea and green tea after 2 p.m.
- Do not eat heavy meals in the evening. Avoid after-dinner snacking.

Self-Preservation

No one wants to talk about the fear of death, which is deeply rooted in us. Self-preservation also manifests in the fear of aging, fear of losing the loved ones and fear of losing worldly possessions such as your house and job. Fear is not merely about physical death. Fear comes from the death of a false self-identity. If you have the self-image of being young and healthy for the rest of your life, this starts falling apart, when you discover your first gray hair. If you want to create a larger than life self-image of your manhood, then you will feel attacked if someone questions your ability to park a car. While the gender battle over the ability to park a car may be amusing, this is a serious attack for a strong self-identity. Such attacks on the self-identity are experienced exactly like the threat of a physical death. The death of a self-identity is probably more painful than a natural physical death. Natural death is like falling asleep. Sleep is known as *sahodara*, the "little sister" of death. You might have a physically painful death if you die of unnatural causes, such as an accident or drowning, but the process of separation itself is not physically painful.

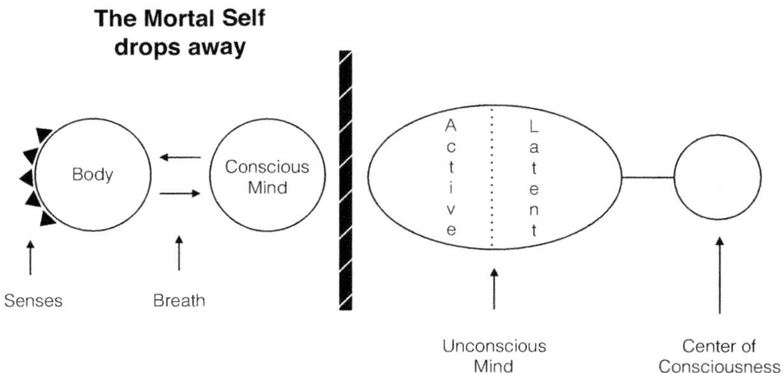

Figure 9.1 **Death is Separation**

When a very old person dies, one says: "You do not have to feel sad because she led a very rich and fulfilling life." On the other hand, when someone dies young, one says: "It is tragic, he was so young, he had so much to live for." A long and fulfilling life means you are able to live out your desires and samskaras but at some point of time the body gets tired. You, Pure Consciousness, have associated with the *nashvar*, "the perishable." You forget that you have attached yourself to the perishable. You do not remember that you are Pure Consciousness, that you are not going to die, that you will come back again and enjoy this all over again, as long as you have the desire. We perceive separation from this body, this plane of existence and from our loved ones as painful (Fig. 9.1). Every time you go through the process of separation you experience that same pain. After innumerable times of experiencing this pain of separation, it becomes deeply etched in your ancient memories. The fear of death or separation is a *vasana*, a diffuse memory of deep fear mixed with a numb pain. You do not remember all these deaths or separations; you are only left with this unknown fear. The fear of death has been learned over innumerable lives, but it can be unlearned.

When you know your eternal nature through direct experience, then you know that you are not really dying. You become fearless. Fearlessness means you are no longer attached to this plane of existence, the "nashvar," because you know through direct experience that you, Pure Consciousness, are eternal and imperishable.

This brings us to the question: How can one regulate the primitive urge of self-preservation? No doubt, this is the most difficult of all the four primitive urges to regulate, since we completely suppress the fear of death.

Approach the primitive urge of self-preservation with respect. Take up at least one of the following exercises:

- Make a list of all your fears, such as fear of loneliness and fear of aging.
- Make your last will and testament.

- Contemplate on what you would do with your life if you were to die in a year.
- Do something every day that gets you out of your comfort zone, like talking to a stranger or asking someone to do you a favor.

The Four Primitive Urges and Awareness

You can gently regulate the four primitive urges. However, when one of the four primitive urges has become completely dominant and taken over your life, you need to get back in charge. For example, excessive consumption of sugar can lead to extreme obesity, diabetes and innumerable other health related issues. Under the circumstances, it might be necessary to completely cut out refined sugar from the diet. This is known as *tyaga* or "abstinence." The same is true for alcohol or drug addiction.

Excessive indulgence in sexual desires is harmful for physical as well as mental hygiene. There is a long tradition of celibacy in spiritual and religious traditions throughout the world. Celibacy is a form of tyaga. Celibacy without mental and spiritual development can be too restrictive and even counterproductive. Celibacy is appropriate only when the person has grown out of the strong physical need and mental desire for sexual satisfaction. Until then, regulation of sexual desires with a steady partner is to be preferred.

To lead a balanced and healthy life, a life of moderation is recommended. You can enjoy sweets and chocolates without forming harmful habits. You may notice that even when the primitive urges are satisfied on a regular basis, still the mind tends to remain preoccupied with thoughts of sex, food, sleep or self-preservation. This shows the clear connection of these primitive urges to the emotional level.

The hold that most of the primitive urges have on you diminishes with increasing age: you need less food and sleep, and the sexual desire is not as strong. This leads many to believe that the practice of advanced pranayama would be easier with age. This may not be necessarily true. It seems a strong foundation in practice is required, else it is very difficult with increasing age to unlearn deep-rooted habit patterns. Also, the primitive urge of self-preservation begins to get really active as the body ages.

In most cases, regulation of the four primitive urges is to be preferred to tyaga. With self-awareness and sensitivity to subtle differences, you will observe that the four primitive urges are interconnected. When one of the four primitive urges is strictly managed, the others become active in an effort to compensate. The primitive urge of self-preservation is so deeply buried that one often remains completely unaware of it. The urge for self-preservation is so basic and primitive that most of us cannot get a handle on it at all. Sleep is hard to observe, since we lose our awareness totally. Sex is deeply connected with strong emotions and social taboos, which makes it difficult to observe and regulate in the beginning. This leaves us with food, as the easiest primitive urge to observe as well as regulate. It is not without a reason that so much emphasis is put on good food as well as regular habits related to food.

As you become more aware of your lifestyle and the primitive urges, you will realize that discipline is not so difficult after all. In fact, awareness and discipline will help you really enjoy your life.

Q&A

Question: I practice a yogic technique called Yoga Nidra to go directly to deep sleep. Since I do not need to dream anymore, I need only 2–3 hours of rest everyday. Please comment.

Answer: Dreaming less is possible only when a systematic method of practice over a long period of time leads to dhyana and the meditator has conscious access to the unconscious mind. The adept brings the unconscious mind forward into waking consciousness and there is less stuff to deal with in the dream state. Through some yogic practices one can learn to go directly to deep sleep, however, there is a difference between a technique and a state. Practicing the technique does not mean you have reached that state. You will learn more about this in Chapter 11 of this book.

Chapter 10

KUMBHAKA, THE ELUSIVE BREATHLESS STATE

Breathlessness should lead to eternal life? Paradoxes like this will challenge your world view, and hopefully even destroy it. Plunge into this deep and vibrant silence, one you have never known before and you will long to return to it. The longing will lead you.

The pranavadins believed that reducing the number of breaths per minute by elongating each breath would correspondingly increase the life span.

If you could elongate your breath to one per minute or maybe even one breath every two minutes and so on, would the life span keep increasing? Could we then say, that as long as the breath is retained within, life would also be retained? Incredible as this sounds, *Kumbhaka* is based on this very principle that has been observed in nature, for instance in animals, and experimented with by generations of pranavadins.

Guiding Principle

Slowing down the breath rate will keep increasing the life span; stopping the breath altogether will keep you alive as long as you can hold your breath.

What is Kumbhaka?

Kumbhaka means "water pot," "jar" or "pitcher." The lungs are like a jar, either they are filled with air or emptied.

Of late Kumbhaka has been practiced by schools based on physical culture. In these physically oriented schools, Kumbhaka is introduced as a breathing exercise; it is practiced as a very violent form of breath retention or breath suspension. These forceful attempts to inhale and retain the breath or to exhale and suspend the breath are harmful, since the body is under tremendous amount of stress and is definitely not relaxed. If the practitioner does not have natural diaphragmatic breathing or a correct posture then the practice of Kumbhaka can cause more harm than benefit to the practitioner. Kumbhaka without preparation can damage the fine tissue of the lungs. Depending on your health condition and the length of retention or suspension, incorrectly practiced Kumbhaka can cause serious harm due to lack of air supply.

There are four variations of Kumbhaka.

Bahya Kumbhaka: Suspension

In this technique the breath is suspended outside the lungs: this means exhalation and then suspension. In effect, the lungs are not filled; you empty the lungs and then suspend the breath. The word *bahya* means "external."

Abhyantara Kumbhaka: Retention

This technique is the opposite of the first. *Abhyantara* means "internal." You fill the lungs and then retain the breath.

Kevala Kumbhaka: Natural Cessation of Breath

This is not really a technique; it is the natural cessation of the breath suddenly and spontaneously. This natural cessation of breath is called Kevala Kumbhaka. This can happen while you are practicing Nadi Shodhanam without Vishnu Mudra, Sushumna Kriya and Sandhya. When the sun and moon are wedded, the energy flows through sushumna leading to Kevala Kumbhaka.

Generally, it is not possible to maintain this form of Kevala Kumbhaka for a longer period of time. It may be experienced by practitioners only momentarily. When the breath stops, even if only for a few moments, you may at first experience a sense of fear.

Breathing is a deep habit. The moment you feel you are not breathing, you panic. Cessation of the breath is deeply associated with death. This fear of death can become a great obstacle. The idea that Kumbhaka can lead to eternal life is, therefore, impossible to grasp without some sort of direct experience.

When natural cessation of the breath occurs more often, the practitioner gradually overcomes the initial fear and realizes that even the subtlest and finest breath is an obstacle. In the few moments of Kevala Kumbhaka, the practitioner experiences utter silence, that gives him a glimpse of the depths of the mind. The practitioner gets frustrated when he cannot maintain the state of joy he experiences in Kevala Kumbhaka, because any effort to forcefully retain the breath creates tension in the body. The mind wrestles with the problem on how to sustain Kevala Kumbhaka for a longer period of time.

Kevala Kumbhaka: The Breathless State

The practitioner has now understood, that if he wants to plunge into the mind and explore its mysteries, he must master Kevala Kumbhaka. The fourth Kumbhaka leads to the breathless state through breath elongation. The fourth Kumbhaka is not spontaneous; it is established through conscious and systematic practice.

This table shows how one can gradually increase breath counts. This is only a suggestion. In this plan the elongated breath is mastered over a period of 30 weeks, i.e. between 7–8 months.

Do not exceed your capacity! If necessary go back to a lower count or spend more than two weeks with a breath count.

Week	Breath Count
1–2	3
3–4	4
5–6	6
7–8	8
9–10	10
11–12	12
13–14	14
15–16	16
17–18	18
19–20	20
21–22	22
23–24	24
25–26	26
27–28	28
29–30	30

Table 10.1 **Equal Breathing**

The breath of an average person is about 2 seconds exhalation and 2 seconds inhalation: this means the average person breathes 15 times per minute. If you elongate your breath gradually to 30 seconds exhalation and 30 seconds inhalation, that would make it just one breath per minute. To do this, just follow the Equal Breathing 7 Month Plan (Table 10.1). Some practitioners may require longer than 7–8 months.

Now imagine you are observing a practitioner exhale and inhale just once every minute: the breath has become so smooth, so silent, so subtle, it seems the practitioner is not breathing. This slowing down of the breath leads to Kevala Kumbhaka. Merely elongating the exhalation and inhalation is not enough since it is difficult to do higher counts in a comfortable and easy manner, once the lung capacity is exhausted. This is only possible if you also eliminate the pause. This is the mysterious revelation in the yogic text, the *Bhagavad Gita 4.29*:

"Still others offer as sacrifice the outgoing breath into the incoming breath, while some offer the incoming breath into the outgoing breath."

This is Sushumna Kriya. Done gradually and systematically with increased elongation of breath and elimination of the pause, Sushumna Kriya leads to Kevala Kumbhaka (Fig. 10.1).

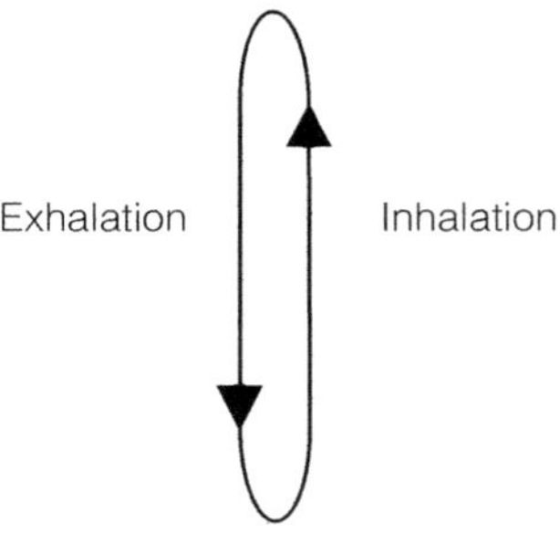

NOTE: Due to the limitations of the illustration this practice may be misunderstood. The illustration may give the impression that you exhale and inhale along the sides of the spine visualizing an oval form. This is not the case. This is not a visualization exercise and both exhalation and inhalation are along the central channel Sushumna, that runs along the spine.

Figure 10.1 **Sushumna Kriya without Pause**

TIP: Elongating the breath does not mean inhaling and exhaling greater quantities of air. Elongating the breath means slowing down the exhalation and inhalation.

Let us consider that after 7–8 months of systematic practice you are able to sustain the elongated breath for 30 seconds exhalation as well as inhalation. If you can sustain the elongated breath for 10 minutes, then you breathe only 10 times instead of the average 150 times. If you can sustain this elongated breath for 15 minutes, then you breathe only 15 times instead of the average 225 times. If you can sustain this elongated breath for 30 minutes, then you breathe only 30 times instead of the average 450 times. Then, as the *Yoga Sutras II.49* explain:

"This having been accomplished, pranayama, which is cessation of inspiration and expiration, follows."

You enter into the deep and profound silence of the breathless state. The flood gates of wisdom open and subtle insights pour in. What seems like hours to an external observer, may seem like time standing still to the one who can sustain Kumbhaka, because Kevala Kumbhaka is not just a breathless state. It is also a timeless state.

Understanding Kevala Kumbhaka

Kevala Kumbhaka is only interesting if you want to plunge into the depths of the mind. If you are not interested in unravelling the mysteries of the mind, then you do not need to understand and experience Kevala Kumbhaka.

Imagine you are standing at a beach watching the waves of the ocean coming towards you. The waves are exhalation and inhalation. The wave is an exhalation as it recedes away from you and an inhalation as it floods towards you. You want to dive into the ocean, so you start walking towards it. You experience this exhalation and inhalation as you stand at the edge of the ocean. As you wade into the water, the water comes to your hips. You do not experience the waves, that is the exhalation and inhalation, as you did at the beach; instead you perceive the waves as a choppy movement of water. You go still deeper into the ocean, until the water comes to your shoulders. You no longer see the waves that you have left behind you, that is, you do not really perceive the exhalation and the inhalation as you are bobbing up and down in the ocean. The exhalation and inhalation that you experienced at the beach was like the average 15 breaths per minute. But now the breath has slowed down to 1 breath per minute, you perceive only the smooth movement of the body of water itself.

Now, you dive into the water. You are no longer on the surface. You are deep inside the ocean. There are no waves. There is no movement. There is no exhalation and no inhalation. This is Kevala Kumbhaka. If you were a fish, you could breathe underwater and stay there indefinitely. So what is the nature of the sea you have dived into? This is the Ocean of Prana, its nature is life itself. A fish does not drown in water because water is its element. So also, you will not drown in the Ocean of Prana, because life is your element. You can sustain Kevala Kumbhaka for a longer period of time without harm, provided it is effortless to maintain and there is absolutely no force or tension involved. Kevala Kumbhaka leads to the direct experience of prana itself.

What happens if you dive into the Ocean of Prana or Pure Consciousness? You do not die. In fact, you unravel the mystery of life and death. You realize through direct experience that the physical plane of consciousness is limited and gross compared to the subtler levels of consciousness you now have access to.

The Five Koshas: The Yogic Body

Just as modern medicine has studied the physical body, the pranavadins studied the gross and subtle energies of the body and mapped these. One of the more detailed pranic maps is that of the nadis and the chakras. There is, however, a more general study of the pranic anatomy. This study explains that there are five *koshas* or "layers." You are not just body and mind. You are made up of layers (Fig. 10.2).

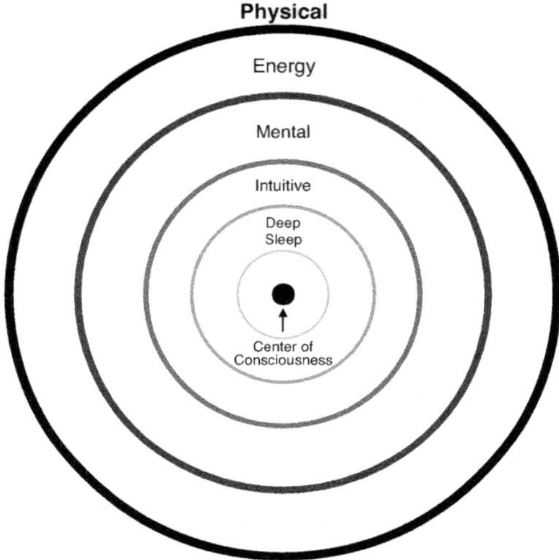

Figure 10.2 **Koshas**

Annamaya Kosha, the Physical Layer

The first layer is *Annamaya* Kosha. *Anna* means "food." *Annamaya* means "composed of food" or "filled with food." While this is a direct reference to the physical body, it includes the world around us. The body itself is just as gross as the worldly objects around us. The entire world is part of this first layer. Materialists remain focused on this layer of the body and worldly objects. Those who practice a style of Yoga based entirely on body culture remain at this first layer.

Pranamaya Kosha, the Energy Layer

The second layer of the individual is *Pranamaya* Kosha. *Pranamaya* means "filled with prana." This is the layer in which the nadis nourish the body. Just as the physical body has the nervous system, the pranic layer of body has nadis, the subtle energy channels that run through the body. These are a subtler form of the nervous system. It is the difference between electric wiring and the electricity that runs through it. While the nerves can be compared to electric wires, the nadis are the concentrated form of energy moving along pranic pathways. There may be blocks in these energy channels; an important part of the practice is to remove these blocks and allow the energy to flow freely through the body.

Blocks in the energy field may manifest at the physical level in the form of disease. Understanding the koshas helps us to heal ourselves. As one begins the inner journey the practitioner travels from the grosser to the subtler layers of the body and in the process stumbles about the pranic blockages. To heal a disease at a physical level you have to go to the pranic level, that is, a layer deeper, to release the block and facilitate healing. A physical disease treated at a physical level may ameliorate suffering, but it cannot remove the cause of the disease. As long as the root cause is not dealt with, the disease will keep manifesting in different forms at different levels.

Manomaya Kosha, the Mental Layer

The third layer is *Manomaya* Kosha. The word *manomaya* means "filled with mind." This is the layer of the mind. While creative and dynamic people have unconsciously gained access to the tremendous potential of the mind, the practitioner seeks to explore the mind consciously and systematically.

Vijnanamaya Kosha, the Layer of Wisdom

The fourth layer is *Vijnanamaya* Kosha. *Vijnana* means "direct knowledge" or "practical knowledge." This is the seat of wisdom known as *buddhi*. Vijnanamaya Kosha is often translated as intellect. This is an incorrect translation because this kosha is not related merely to reasoning. It is an extremely subtle layer, and therefore difficult to relate to without direct experience. Having access to

Vijnanamaya Kosha means the practitioner is guided by his inner voice of wisdom and he is no longer dependent on external guidance. He is well on his way to becoming an adept.

Anandamaya Kosha, the Layer of Joy and Bliss

The fifth layer is *Anandamaya* Kosha. *Anandamaya* means "filled with joy." You go into deep sleep every night, but you do so unconsciously. If you would experience deep sleep consciously, you would experience absolute bliss or pure joy known as Ananda. The idea of experiencing deep sleep consciously seems paradoxical. How can one be in deep sleep and yet conscious? As you go deeper into the subtler realms you will encounter apparently paradoxical situations where the laws of the external world do not hold.

The koshas are connected to the Center of Consciousness by Adi Prana. This is no longer just the nadis but the source of all energy. To use the example of electricity, this is not just the electric wiring in the house, but the main cable carrying the electricity from a nuclear reactor to a city. The Center of Consciousness is like the nuclear reactor, which is the source of all energy.

These koshas are like the waves in the Ocean of Prana, that is why they are generally visualized as ripples around a drop. There are five rings around a dot of Pure Consciousness. The outmost ring is the Annamaya Kosha. The innermost ring, the Anandamaya Kosha, is called Deep Sleep. The drop is the Center of Consciousness, the source of all energy or prana.

Piercing the Five Layers

The concept of margas, in relation to the yogic anatomy, has already been explained in Chapter 8. This concept is also used in relation to the five koshas.

Nivritti Marga

The process of moving from the gross to the subtle is known as Nivritti Marga. Through systematic practice, you allow your attention to move from the body to the layer of energy, go deeper into the mind and get in touch with your inner wisdom. Eventually, systematic practice will lead you to the Anandamaya Kosha, the deepest sheath of pure joy and bliss (Fig. 10.3).

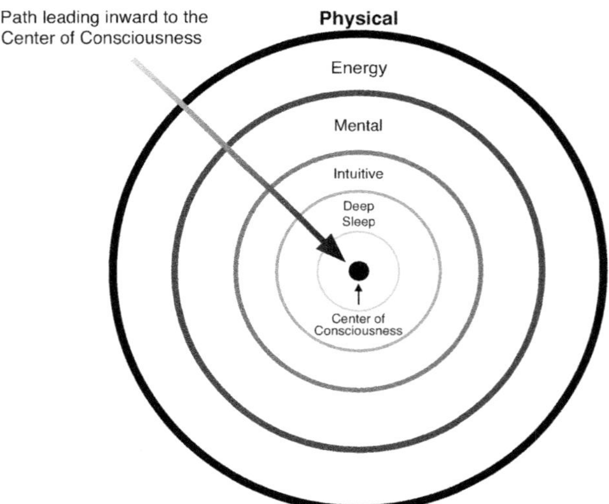

Figure 10.3 **Nivritti Marga**

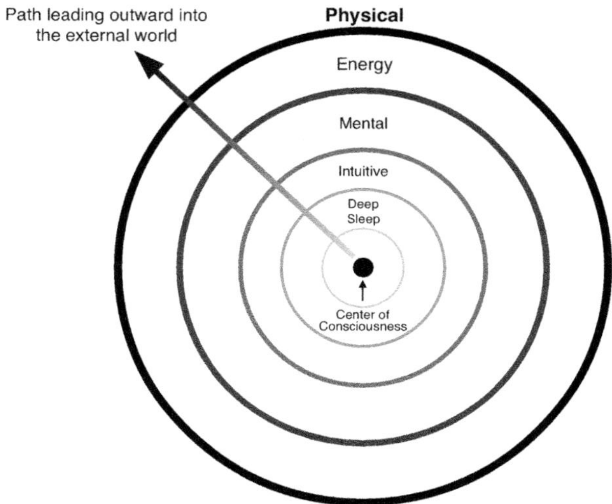

Figure 10.4 **Pravritti Marga**

Pravritti Marga

The koshas are nothing other than waves of energy, which create the body and the world. They emerge from a drop of Pure Consciousness and expand outward like a ripple. This is how consciousness radiates outward, manifesting the body and the world. Pravritti Marga is the path of evolution and it happens naturally and effortlessly (Fig. 10.4), while the path of dissolution or Nivritti Marga requires effort and practice. Materialists emphasize on the outward moving path, while spiritualists emphasize on the inward moving path. In reality both the paths are incomplete.

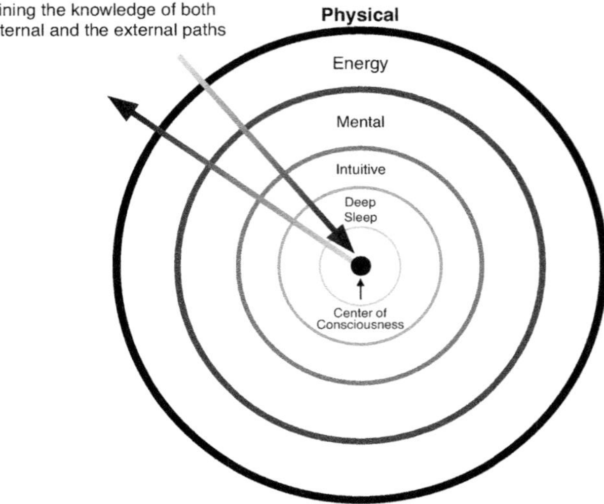

Figure 10.5 **Purna Marga**

Purna Marga

Mastery is attained when you can do both, systematically go inward as well as return to the external world (Fig. 10.5). You neither reject the world as many spiritualists and religionists do, nor do you reject the subtler realms as many materialists and scientists do.

In the following chapter you will learn how to master both Nivritti Marga as well as Pravritti Marga, that is, go to the deeper realms and emerge again. It is like diving deep into the water, enjoying the deep silence and stillness and returning to the surface to enjoy the world.

Chapter 11

THE MYSTERIOUS FOURTH PRANAYAMA

After uninterrupted practice over a long period of time something odd happens. It seems, all the practices start merging and lead to one and the same place, a place of reasonless joy and profound beauty. The fourth pranayama is the direct experience of prana itself.

This chapter introduces advanced pranayama practices. These practices can take you to Adi Prana itself, provided the systematic method has been followed and all other factors, specially lifestyle, have been taken into consideration.

General Guidelines

Do these practices in a quiet and dark room. If you live in a busy neighborhood, then you might want to do these practices in the early hours of the morning after a good night's sleep, and before the world around you gets active and busy. Practicing after a good night's sleep means you are well rested and will not fall asleep. It is preferable to do these practices when it is still dark. You may do these practices at night, provided you are not tired and will not fall asleep. If you are falling asleep, then snap out of it, go through the practice quickly and end it.

TIP: Do not form the habit of falling asleep. These practices are meant to awaken you to the deeper mysteries of life, not put you to sleep.

Most of these practices are done in the supine position. Lie down on your back with the support of your hands. Keep the arms away from the body and keep the palms of the hands facing upward. The legs should not be too far apart and the feet should be relaxed. When the practice is over, do not get up abruptly from the supine posture. Always turn to the left and rise up using the support of the left arm.

Do not do these practices when you are tired, chances are that you will fall asleep. For the same reason, you should not do these practices on a full stomach. These practices are best done before meals.

Do not lie down on the bare floor or a thin yoga mat. For these practices you require a thin mattress that is not too bouncy or soft. The head should be supported by a flat pillow. You may require a warm blanket to cover yourself so that you do not feel cold. Do not do these practices on your bed, since the bed is associated with sleep. You may want to use a thin hat or a shawl to cover your eyes; this is only required if you are practicing during the day and cannot darken the room entirely.

Counting causes jerks in the breath and prevents the practitioner from focusing on the deep and long flow of the breath; therefore use the body itself to measure the length of the breath.

Do not do these practices outdoors or in places you do not feel safe and secure.

Aum Kriya

Aum Kriya is a simple practice for Equal Breathing in the supine position. It is subtler than the Equal Breathing practice in the seated position. However, it is not advisable to skip the seated variation and start directly with the supine version, since experience has shown that most practitioners fall asleep in the supine position. Train the Equal Breathing practice in the seated position for 7–8 months as explained in Chapter 4 before you start with these subtler and finer practices. The first three variations of the practice help you to steadily and gradually elongate the breath and make it finer. They are a preparation for Aum Kriya.

Variation 1: Equal Breath short

Exhale slowly as the awareness travels from the Sahasrara Chakra to the Muladhara Chakra in a straight line along the spine. Then inhale and allow the attention to travel gradually from the Muladhara Chakra to the Sahasrara Chakra (Fig. 11.1). Allow the exhalation to flow into the inhalation and the inhalation to flow into the exhalation without any pauses.

This practice is no different from Equal Breathing in the seated position. It is just a little more comfortable and you can do it for longer periods of time without getting tired.

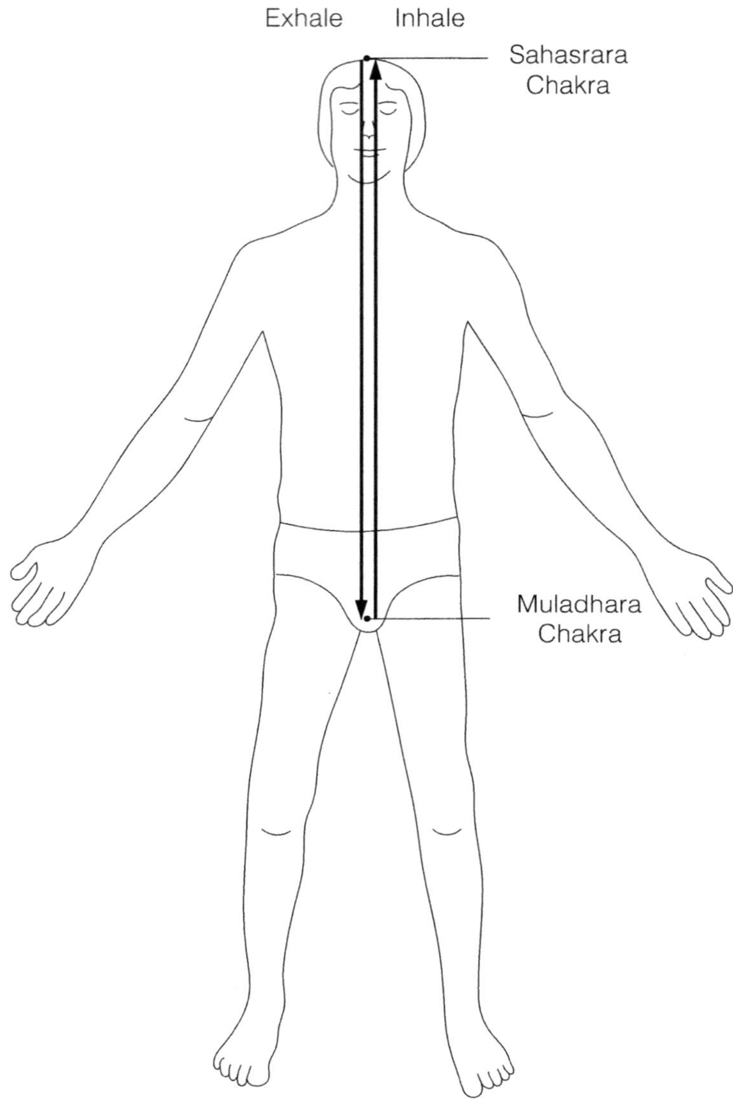

Figure 11.1 **Aum Kriya Variation 1 – Equal Breath Short**

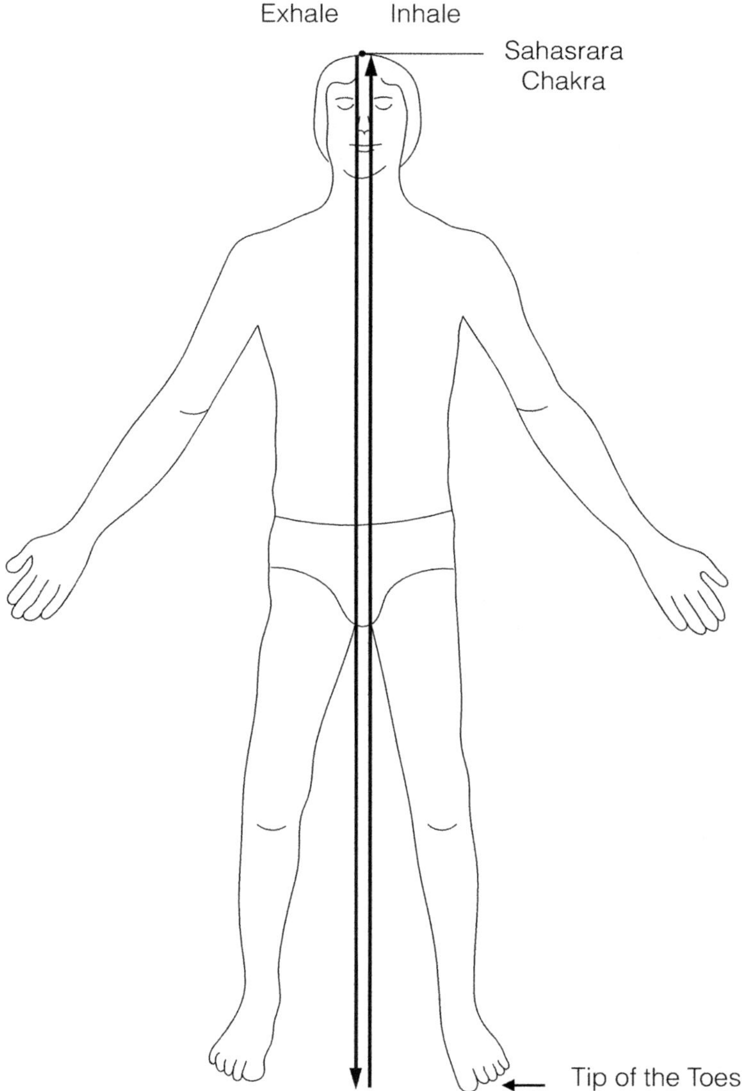

Figure 11.2 **Aum Kriya Variation 2 – Equal Breath Long**

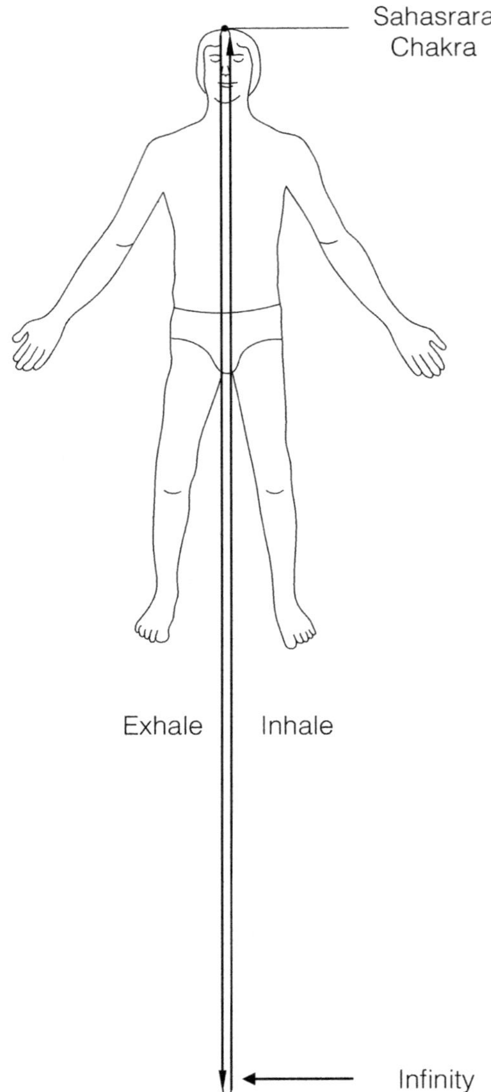

Figure 11.3 **Aum Kriya Variation 3 – Equal Breath Elongated**

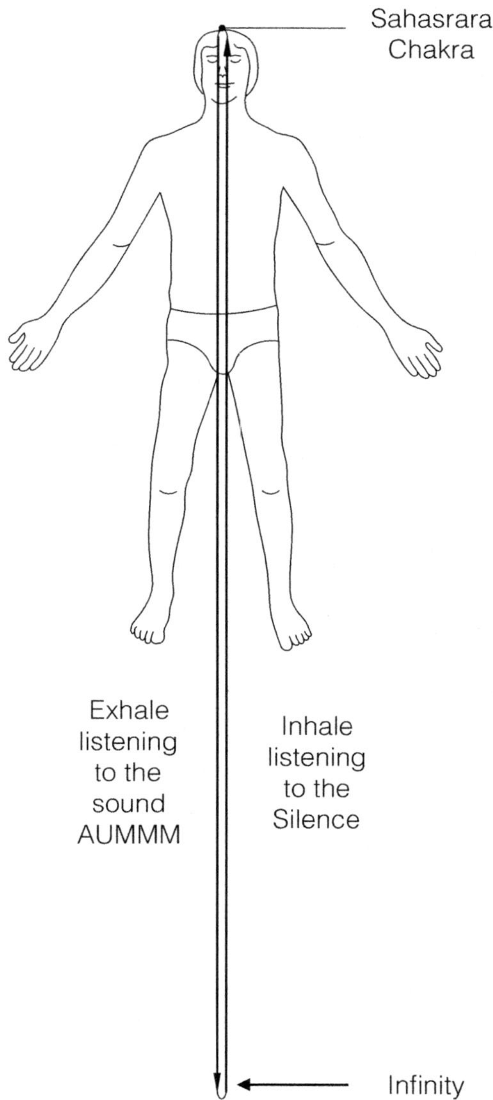

Figure 11.4 **Aum Kriya Variation 4**

Variation 2: Equal Breath long

Exhale slowly as the attention travels from the Sahasrara Chakra to the tip of the toes in a straight line along the spine. Do not keep the legs too far apart in this practice. Then inhale and allow the attention to travel gradually from the tip of the toes to the Sahasrara Chakra (Fig. 11.2). Allow the exhalation to flow into the inhalation and the inhalation to flow into the exhalation without any pauses.

Spend a couple of months doing this practice, allowing the breath to elongate effortlessly.

Variation 3: Equal Breath elongated

Exhale slowly. As the attention travels downward from the Sahasrara Chakra in a straight line along the spine, allow it to go as far as it can. It feels as though the attention can travel into infinity. Breathe in from infinity and allow the attention to travel very slowly in a straight line along the spine to the Sahasrara Chakra (Fig. 11.3). Allow the exhalation to flow into the inhalation and the inhalation to flow into the exhalation without any pauses.

This practice will help elongating the breath to your maximum capacity.

Variation 4: Equal Breath with Aum

Once you have been doing Variation 3 for a couple of months, you can do the same with the mantra Aum. Listen mentally to the sound Aum when you exhale; listen to the silence when you inhale (Fig. 11.4). Always allow the exhalation to flow into the inhalation and the inhalation to flow into the exhalation without any pauses.

The *Yoga Sutras* explain that the respiration must be very subtle (*suksma*) and elongated (*dirgha*) to directly experience the fourth pranayama or prana itself. This practice promotes a subtle and elongated breath.

TIP: If you do Aum Kriya correctly, the breath may stop spontaneously and naturally. If that happens, there is no reason to be afraid or to stop the practice. This natural cessation of the breath is Kevala Kumbhaka and it is a sign of progress.

Shavyatra

Shavyatra is a relatively easy practice that can be done every day. If you have practiced systematically and are proficient in Nadi Shodhanam, Sushumna Kriya and Sandhya Kriya, then you can start directly with Variation 3 of Shavyatra.

Variation 3: 61 points

In this practice the attention travels through the body, resting at 61 points from the head, to the right arm, the left arm, torso, right leg, left leg and back to the head. This is a journey through the body. This is what Shavyatra literally means; *shava* means "corpse" and *yatra* is "journey."

Lie down on the floor as specified in the general guidelines. Keep the eyes gently closed and allow the lips, hands and feet to be relaxed. Watch the diaphragm raise and fall 10 times becoming aware of the fine, deep breath without noise, jerks or pauses (Fig. 11.5).

1. Turn your attention to the space between the eyebrows. This is the Ajna Chakra. Let your attention rest there for a couple of seconds.
2. Let the attention travel to the Vishuddha Chakra, the Throat Center at the pit of the throat
3. The right shoulder joint
4. The right elbow joint

5. The right wrist joint
6. The tip of the right thumb
7. The tip of the right forefinger
8. The tip of the right middle finger
9. The tip of the right ring finger
10. The tip of the right little finger
11. Let the attention return to the right wrist joint
12. The right elbow joint
13. The right shoulder joint
14. Let the attention travel back to Vishuddha Chakra, the Throat Center at the pit of the throat
15. The left shoulder joint
16. The left elbow joint
17. The left wrist joint
18. The tip of the left thumb
19. The tip of the left forefinger
20. The tip of the left middle finger
21. The tip of the left ring finger
22. The tip of the left little finger
23. The left wrist joint
24. The left elbow joint
25. The left shoulder joint
26. Let the attention travel back to Vishuddha Chakra, the Throat Center at the pit of the throat
27. Let the attention travel down to Anahata Chakra, the Heart Center between the breasts
28. The right breast
29. The Heart Center again

30. The left breast
31. The Heart Center again
32. The Manipura Chakra, the Navel Center
33. The center of the abdomen
34. The right hip joint
35. The right knee joint
36. The right ankle joint
37. The tip of the right big toe
38. The tip of the right second toe
39. The tip of the right third toe
40. The tip of the right fourth toe
41. The tip of the right little toe
42. The right ankle joint
43. The right knee joint
44. The right hip joint
45. The center of the abdomen
46. The left hip joint
47. The left knee joint
48. The left ankle joint
49. The tip of the left big toe
50. The tip of the left second toe
51. The tip of the left third toe
52. The tip of the left fourth toe
53. The tip of the left little toe
54. The left ankle joint
55. The left knee joint
56. The left hip joint

57. The center of the abdomen
58. The Manipura Chakra, the Navel Center
59. Let the attention travel to Anahata Chakra between the breasts
60. Let the attention travel back to Vishuddha Chakra at the pit of the throat
61. Let your attention rest at the Ajna Chakra, the space between the eyebrows

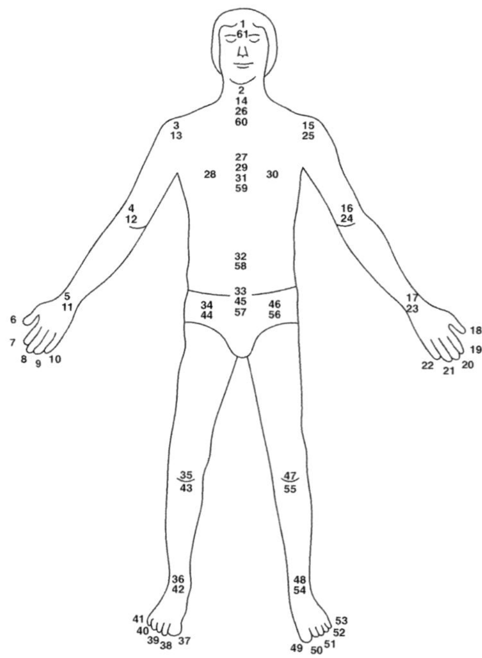

Figure 11.5 **Shavyatra Variation 3 – 61 points**

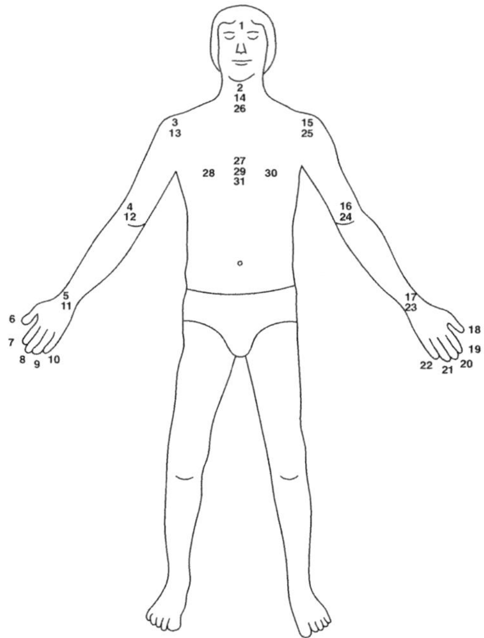

Figure 11.6 **Shavyatra Variation 2 – 31 points**

This practice is not meant to be a difficult concentration exercise, therefore allow your attention to rest gently at the different points. Do not allow the body to get tense. The practice follows a clear pattern through the body and it is best to memorize the journey that the awareness takes through the body.

There is no clearly defined amount of time that you spend at a certain point. You must make sure you do not stay so long at a point that you fall asleep or the mind wanders off. If the mind always wanders off at the same point every time you practice, then it indicates a blockage in the pranic channel. As you come close to this blocked point, do not rest there too long, just go ahead to the next point.

Nyasa and Shavyatra

Shavyatra is a tantric practice known as *Nyasa*. There are many versions of *Nyasa*. Shavyatra, as described here, is the simplest and most effective *Nyasa*. *Nyasa* means "to place," because a divinity is placed at each of the points together with mantra repetition and in this manner the entire body becomes divine and flooded with prana.

The many different visualization versions of Nyasa are complicated. The simpler the exercise, the deeper it goes, since the visualization prevents you from seeing the inner light of prana. If you practice Shavyatra as described here daily over a long period of time, you will see the light of prana emerging from the darkness. This is the fourth pranayama.

Variation 2: 31 points

Locating these points with the help of the mind's eye in the pranic body is a subtle exercise and some may find it difficult. Others are able to locate the points easily but find it hard to hold the attention since the mind keeps wandering off. As a solution for either of these problems, you may practice a shortened version of Shavyatra by focusing only on 31 points (Fig. 11.6). Practice the 31 points exercise for a couple of weeks before you go back to the 61 points technique.

Lie down on the floor in the prescribed manner. Keep the eyes gently closed and allow the lips, hands and feet to be relaxed. Watch the abdomen rise and fall 10 times becoming aware of the fine, deep breath without noise, jerks or pauses.

1. Turn your attention to the space between the eyebrows. This is the Ajna Chakra. Let your attention rest there for a couple of seconds.
2. Let the attention travel to the Vishuddha Chakra, the Throat Center at the pit of the throat

3. The right shoulder joint
4. The right elbow joint
5. The right wrist joint
6. The tip of the right thumb
7. The tip of the right forefinger
8. The tip of the right middle finger
9. The tip of the right ring finger
10. The tip of the right little finger
11. Let the attention return to the right wrist joint
12. The right elbow joint
13. The right shoulder joint
14. Let the attention travel back to Vishuddha Chakra, the Throat Center at the pit of the throat
15. The left shoulder joint
16. The left elbow joint
17. The left wrist joint
18. The tip of the left thumb
19. The tip of the left forefinger
20. The tip of the left middle finger
21. The tip of the left ring finger
22. The tip of the left little finger
23. The left wrist joint
24. The left elbow joint
25. The left shoulder joint
26. Let the attention travel back to Vishuddha Chakra, the Throat Center at the pit of the throat
27. Let the attention travel down to Anahata Chakra, the Heart Center between the two breasts

28. The right breast
29. Return briefly to the Heart Center
30. The left breast
31. Let your attention rest at Anahata Chakra, the Heart Center between the two breasts

Variation 1: Shavasana

Shavasana is a more general version of Shavyatra. Generally, Shavasana is used to recover between strenuous postures or to train diaphragmatic breathing. It is also a preparatory practice for Shavyatra.

Lie on the back as specified in the general guidelines. Do not make suggestions to your body. Observe your body mentally. Your forehead is relaxed, your eyes are gently closed, your mouth and jaws are completely relaxed. Observe the neck and shoulders. Feel the weight of the arms and hands falling to the floor. Allow your attention to return to the shoulders and neck, before you allow it to travel to your chest. Inhale and exhale normally. Let the attention move to the abdominal area. Watch the abdomen raise and fall in your mind's eye. Survey the pelvic area, the hips, the thighs, knees, calves, ankles and feet. Allow your attention to sweep through your body backwards from the feet to the knees and thighs to the hips. Survey the abdomen, chest, neck, and finally returning to the head. Remain in this posture breathing normally 10–15 times, then turn gently to the left side and using the support of your left arm, get up slowly.

Shitalikarana

Shitalikarana comes from the Sanskrit verb, *shitalikaroti*, which means "to cool." The word *shitali* means, among many things, "cool," "calm" and "free from passions." It also means "sandalwood," "moon," "lotus" and "pearl," all of which are known for their cooling qualities. Shitalikarana is not meant to help you sleep, it is meant to make you conscious and aware. There is a possibility that you might fall asleep in the initial attempts at practicing Shitalikarana since it is a rather long practice with a total of 21 steps.

Be mindful of the fact that Steps 2–11 go inward with a shortening of the breath and Steps 12–19 come outward by gradually lengthening the breath. Shitalikarana is an advanced pranayama practice, provided you have followed the 7 Step Program systematically. If this is not the case, chances are that Shitalikarana will remain a mere technique because it will be difficult to shorten the breath and to maintain a smooth and subtle breath.

How to practice Shitalikarana

Lie on the back as specified in the general guidelines. Keep the eyes gently closed and allow the lips, hands and feet to be relaxed.

Step 1
Breath diaphragmatically 5 times (Fig. 11.7).

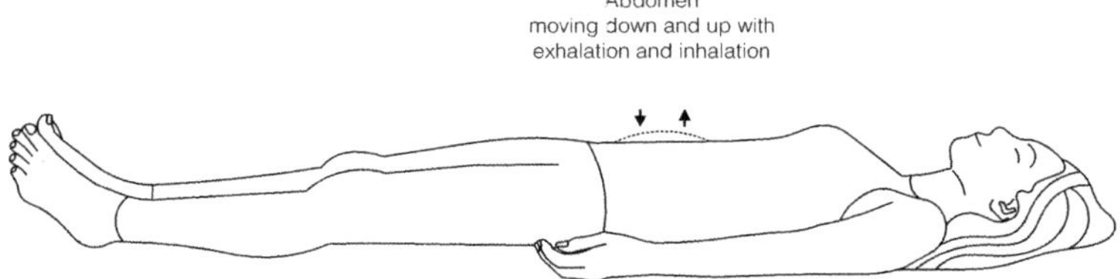

Figure 11.7 **Shitalikarana – Step 1**

Step 2 and Step 19

While exhaling, let your attention travel from Sahasrara Chakra through the Ajna Chakra, the space between the nostrils (Nasagre), the Vishuddha Chakra, Anahata Chakra, Manipura Chakra, Muladhara Chakra, the knees and the ankles to the toes.

While inhaling, let your attention travel from the toes through the ankles, the knees, Muladhara Chakra, Manipura Chakra, Anahata Chakra, Vishuddha Chakra, the space between the nostrils (Nasagre), and the Ajna Chakra to Sahasrara Chakra (Fig. 11.8).

Do this 10 times.

The second chakra, the Svadhisthana Chakra, is deliberately omitted in this practice.

TIP: You do not need to keep counts to measure the length of the breath since the body itself is a measure of the length of the breath.

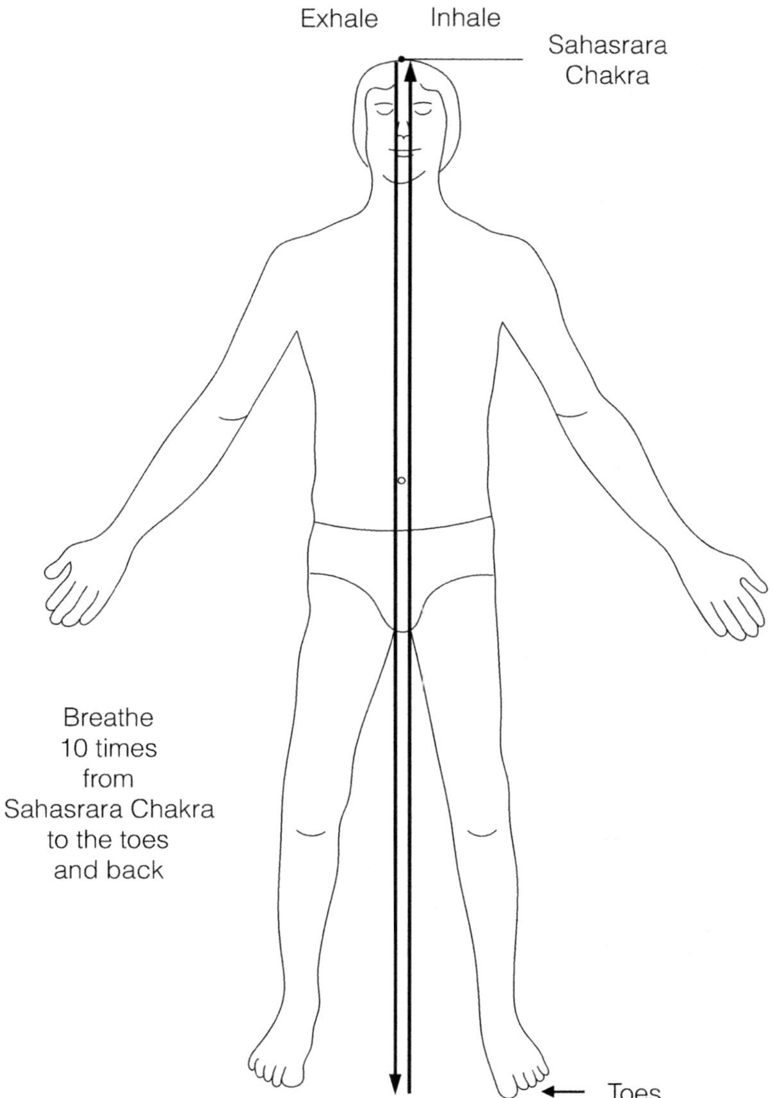

Figure 11.8 **Shitalikarana – Step 2 and 19**

Step 3 and Step 18

While exhaling, let your attention travel from Sahasrara Chakra through the Ajna Chakra, the space between the nostrils (Nasagre), Vishuddha Chakra, Anahata Chakra, Manipura Chakra, Muladhara Chakra and the knees to the ankles.

While inhaling, let your attention travel back from the ankles, the knees, Muladhara Chakra, Manipura Chakra, Anahata Chakra, Vishuddha Chakra, the space between the nostrils (Nasagre) and Ajna Chakra to the Sahasrara Chakra (Fig. 11.9).

Do this 10 times.

TIP: The breath should be smooth and noiseless.

Step 4 and Step 17

While exhaling, let your attention travel from Sahasrara Chakra through Ajna Chakra, Nasagre, Vishuddha Chakra, Anahata Chakra, Manipura Chakra and Muladhara Chakra to the knees.

While inhaling, let your attention travel from the knees, through Muladhara Chakra, Manipura Chakra, Anahata Chakra, Vishuddha Chakra, Nasagre and Ajna Chakra to Sahasrara Chakra (Fig. 11.10).

Do this 10 times.

TIP: Do not stop at all the points mentally, rather allow the attention to flow along the spine smoothly without jerks or pauses.

Step 5 and Step 16

While exhaling, let your attention travel from Sahasrara Chakra through Ajna Chakra, Nasagre, Vishuddha Chakra, Anahata Chakra and Manipura Chakra to Muladhara Chakra.

While inhaling, let your attention travel from Muladhara Chakra through Manipura Chakra, Anahata Chakra, Vishuddha Chakra, Nasagre and Ajna Chakra to Sahasrara Chakra (Fig. 11.11).

Do this 5 times.

Now that the lower limbs are no longer involved in the practice, the attention is focused on the area of the head and along the spinal cord.

Step 6 and Step 15

While exhaling, let your attention travel from Sahasrara Chakra through Ajna Chakra, Nasagre, Vishuddha Chakra and Anahata Chakra to Manipura Chakra.

While inhaling, let your attention travel from Manipura Chakra through Anahata Chakra, Vishuddha Chakra, Nasagre and Ajna Chakra to Sahasrara Chakra (Fig. 11.12).

Do this 5 times.

Step 7 and Step 14

While exhaling, let your attention travel from Sahasrara Chakra through Ajna Chakra, Nasagre and Vishuddha Chakra to Anahata Chakra.

While inhaling, let your attention travel from Anahata Chakra through Vishuddha Chakra, Nasagre and Ajna Chakra to Sahasrara Chakra (Fig. 11.13).

Do this 5 times.

TIP: The duration or length of the inhalation and exhalation is shortening rapidly. Some may experience a bit of discomfort initially. This means that Steps 1–4 have not been done carefully.

Step 8 and Step 13

While exhaling, let your attention travel from Sahasrara Chakra through the Ajna Chakra and Nasagre to Vishuddha Chakra.

While inhaling, let your attention travel from Vishuddha Chakra through Nasagre and Ajna Chakra to Sahasrara Chakra (Fig. 11.14).

Do this 5 times.

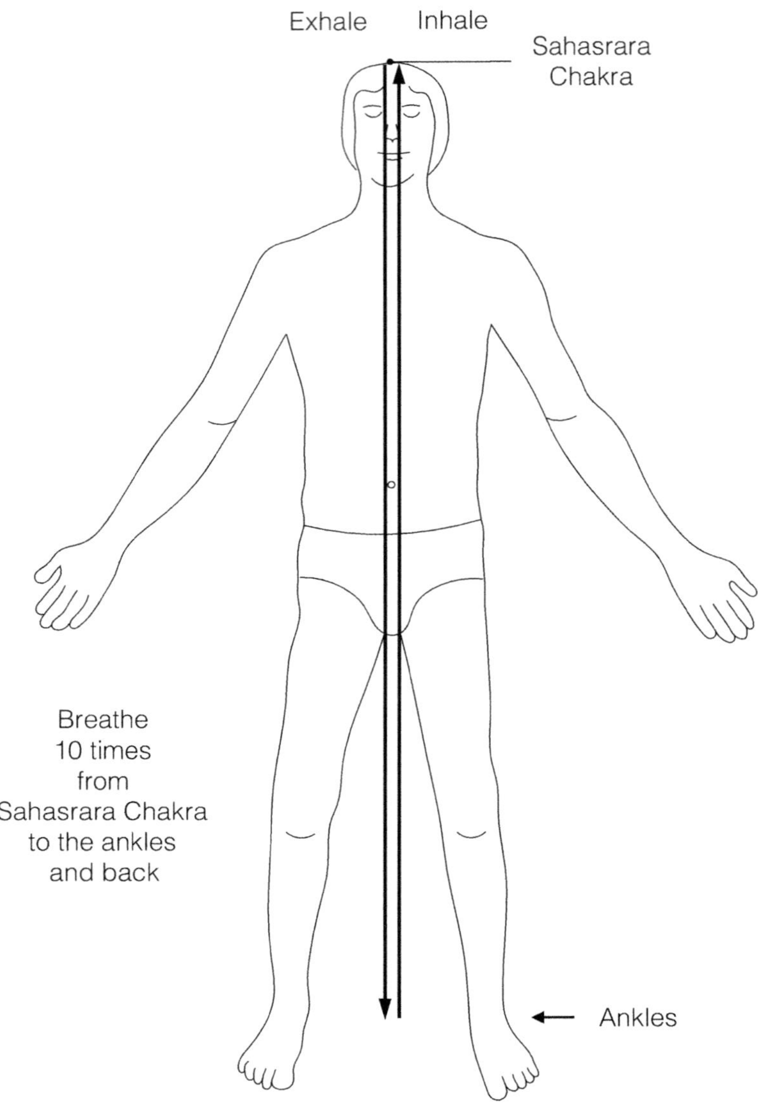

Figure 11.9 **Shitalikarana – Step 3 and 18**

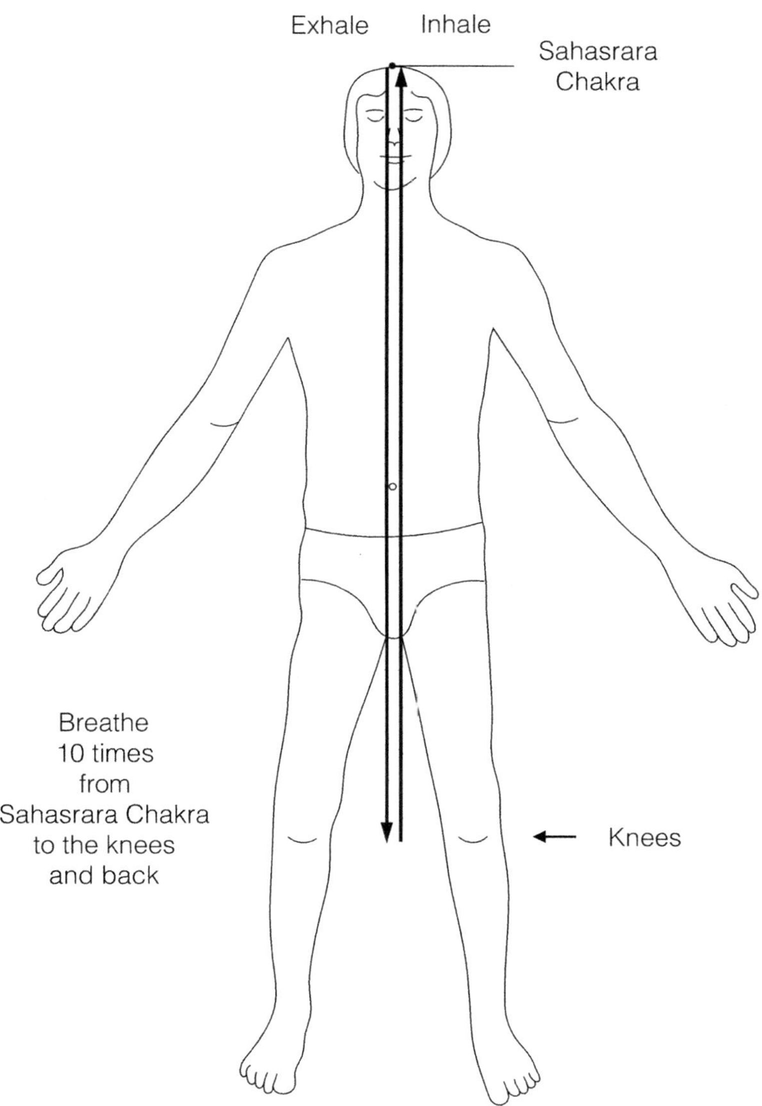

Figure 11.10 **Shitalikarana – Step 4 and 17**

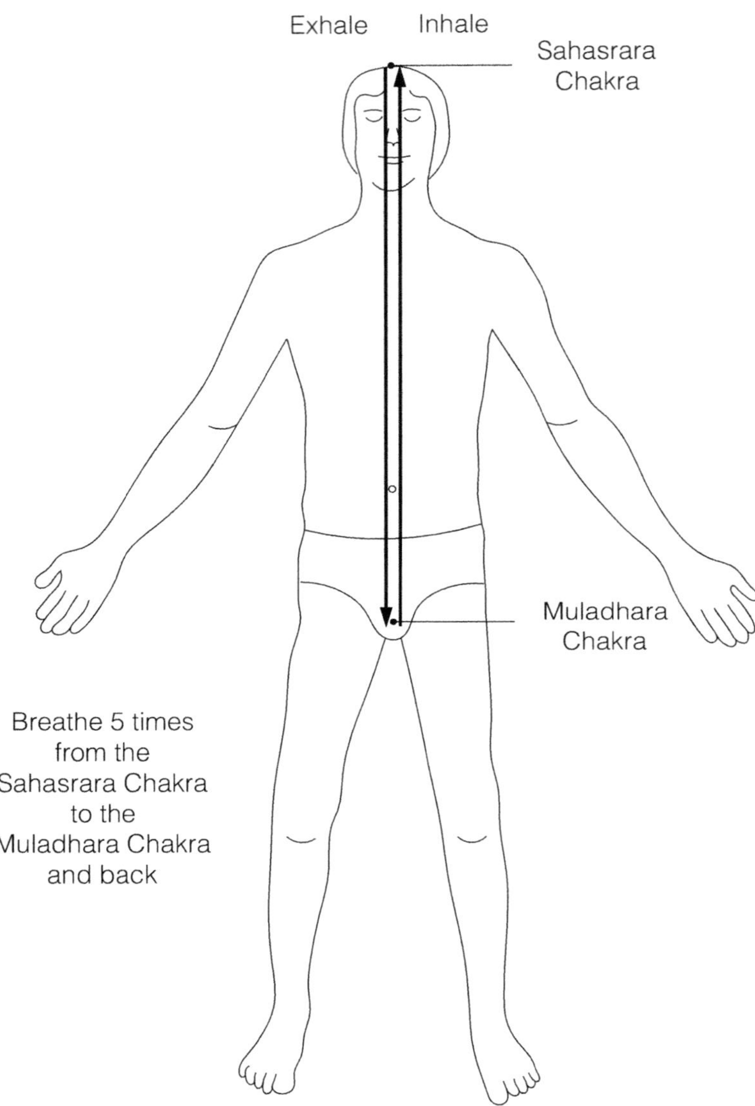

Figure 11.11 **Shitalikarana – Step 5 and 16**

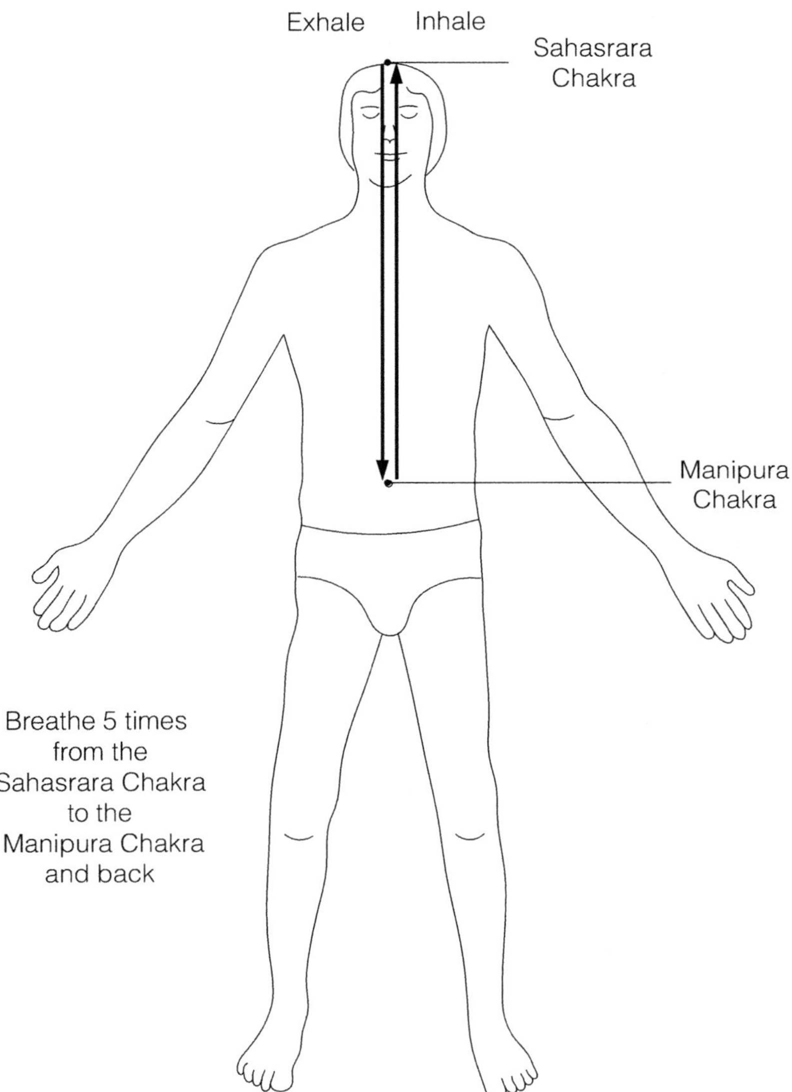

Figure 11.12 **Shitalikarana – Step 6 and 15**

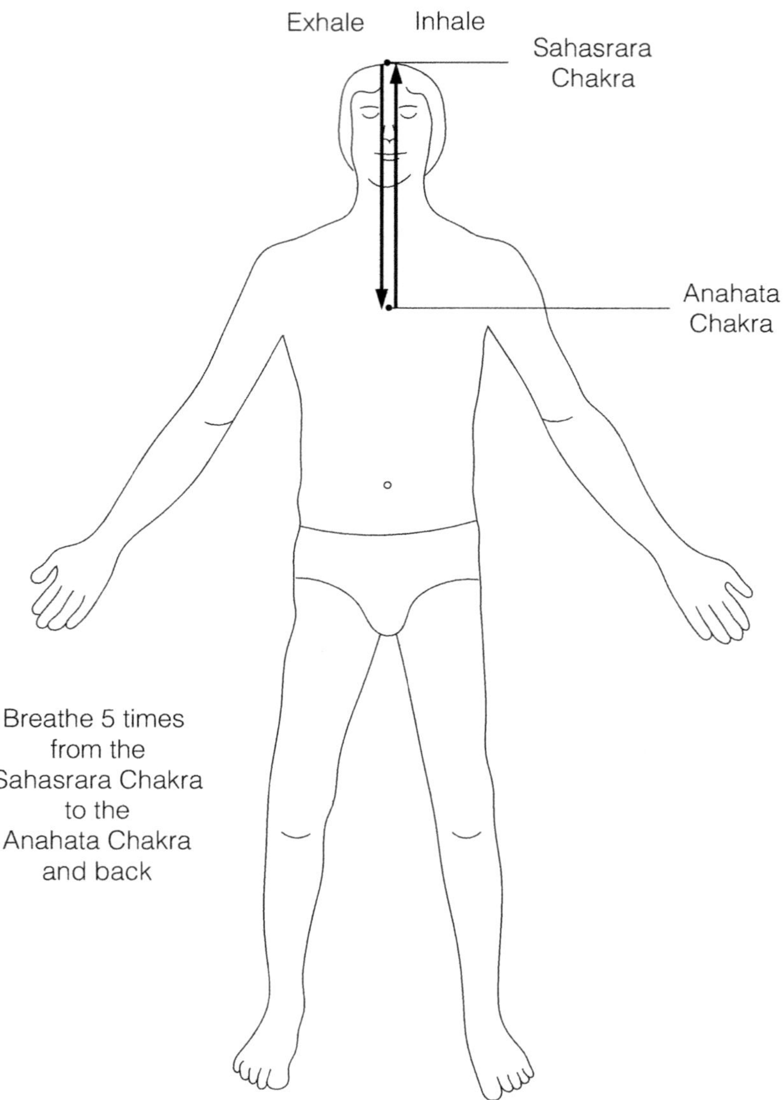

Figure 11.13 **Shitalikarana – Step 7 and 14**

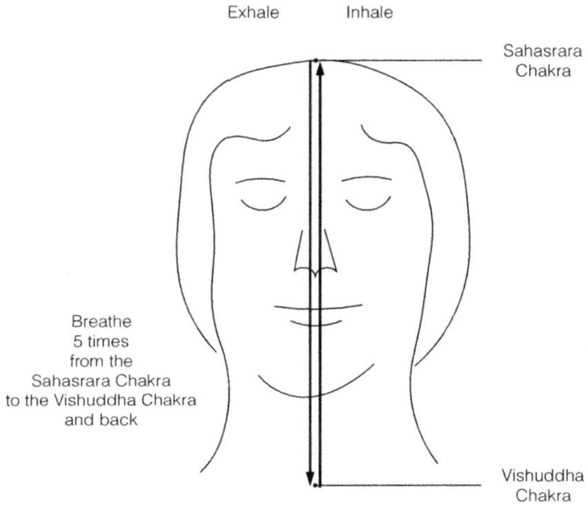

Figure 11.14 **Shitalikarana – Step 8 and 13**

Step 9 and Step 12

While exhaling, let your attention travel from Sahasrara Chakra through Ajna Chakra to Nasagre.

While inhaling, let your attention travel from Nasagre through Ajna Chakra to Sahasrara Chaka (Fig. 11.15).

Do this 5 times.

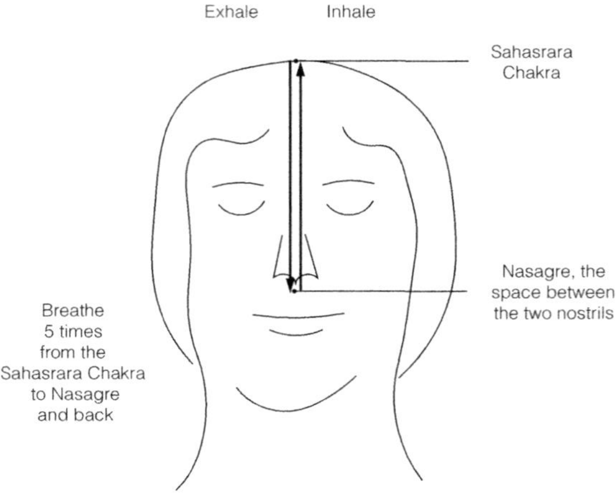

Figure 11.15 **Shitalikarana – Step 9 and 12**

Step 10

Allow the attention to rest at Nasagre, the space between the nostrils. Observe your breath here for around 10 breaths (Fig. 11.16). If one of the nostrils is closed, open it using the power of attention as explained in Sandhya Kriya.

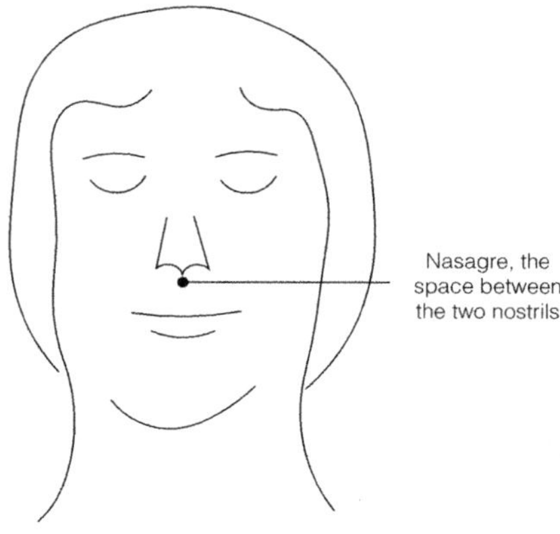

Allow the attention to rest at Nasagre. Observe your breath here for around 10 breaths. If one of your nostrils is closed, open it using the power of attention.

Figure 11.16 **Shitalikarana – Step 10**

TIP: Make sure you do not fall asleep.

Step 11

Let your attention rest at the Ajna Chakra for 10 breaths or as long as it is comfortable (Fig. 11.17).

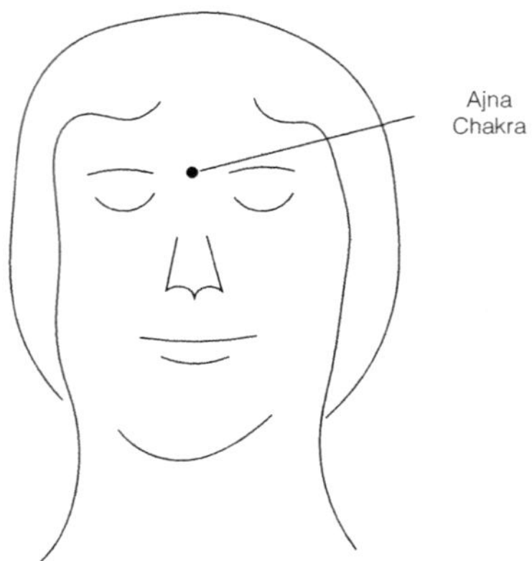

Allow the attention to rest at the Ajna Chakra for around 10 breaths or as long as comfortable.

Figure 11.17 **Shitalikarana – Step 11**

TIP: You may suddenly find that the breath stops. Do not be afraid; this is Kevala Kumbhaka.

Now return outward by lengthening the breath in Steps 12–19.

Step 20

Turn slowly to your left side. While exhaling, let your attention travel from the head to the toes; while inhaling, let your attention travel from the toes to the head. Breathe as if your right side is exhaling and inhaling. Do this 10 times.

Turn slowly to your right side. While exhaling let your attention travel from the head to the toes and while inhaling let your attention travel from the toes to the head. Breathe as if your left side is exhaling and inhaling. Do this 10 times.

The heart is rested completely and the body may seem to be inert. This feeling will pass. Do not move abruptly or get up suddenly. This may disturb the subtle pranic vehicles.

Step 21
Get up with the support of your hands or turn on your back and practice Yoga Nidra.

When you do Shitalikarana often enough, you notice that in Steps 2–11 the breath is shortened instead of elongated. The shortening of breath leads to Kumbhaka. It leads you within. This is Nivritti Marga, the inward path. Steps 11–21 elongate the breath, leading back into the world; this is Pravritti Marga, the outward path. Once you start the inward path, that is the shortening of the breath, it is important to complete the outward path, that is the elongation of the breath, else you may shock the nervous system. This is Purna Marga, the complete path.

Yoga Nidra

Yoga Nidra is a technique as well as a state of consciousness. The Sanskrit word *nidra* means "sleep." The state of Yoga Nidra is an advanced state of consciousness, in which Pure Consciousness shines through the darkness of deep sleep. In this state one experiences complete awareness and absolute bliss. While you may practice the technique of Yoga Nidra, it may or may not lead you to the state of Yoga Nidra, depending on many factors, such as regularity of practice, intensity of desire, lifestyle, etc.

Variation 1: Short version without preparation

In this practice you use the breath as a thread to connect the three points of concentration, Ajna Chakra, Vishuddha Chakra and Anahata Chakra.

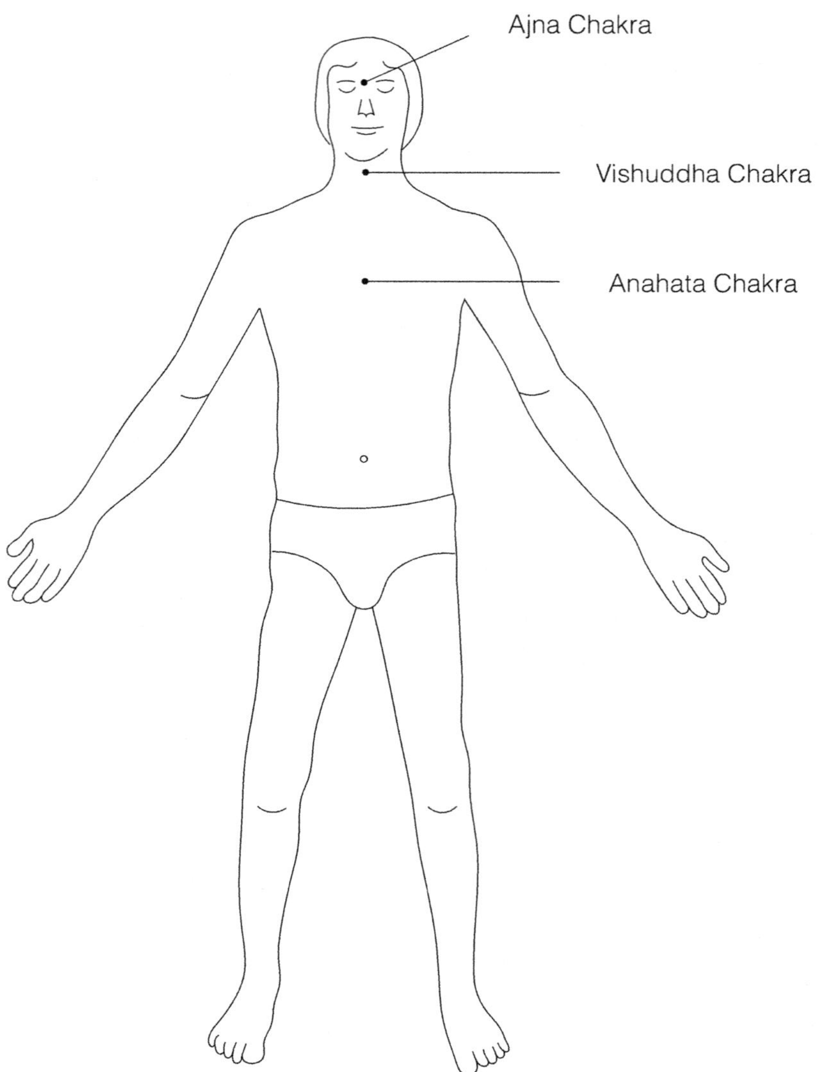

Figure 11.18 **Yoga Nidra**

Lie on a thin mattress as described in the general guidelines. Close your eyes gently. Let your awareness be gently focused at the Ajna Chakra between the eyebrows (Fig. 11.18). Be aware of your breath all the time, while keeping the focus of your attention at the space between the eyebrows.

Gently allow your attention to shift to the Vishuddha Chakra with the help of your breath. If you want, you may visualize the moon at the Vishuddha Chakra. You may notice that some images emerge spontaneously and effortlessly. In this case, make sure that you do not fall asleep. Breathe naturally and diaphragmatically, but remember to keep your attention at the Vishuddha Chakra and not at the diaphragm.

After a few breaths allow your attention to shift to Anahata Chakra. Allow your attention to rest at this focal point. The breath will become very fine and you may start falling asleep. Be aware of the threshold of sleep. Do not let yourself fall asleep. It is not recommended to do this practice for longer than 10 minutes. Now reverse the process. Allow your attention to shift to the Vishuddha Chakra and Ajna Chakra with the help of your breath. Open your eyes gently.

Variation 2: Longer version with preparation

The longer variation includes the preparatory practices of Shavyatra and Shitalikarana. Practice the following sequence in a darkened room or in the early hours of the morning:

- Shavyatra
- Shitalikarana
- Yoga Nidra

The short variation is the actual Yoga Nidra practice and is suitable only for adepts. The long variation is recommended, since it includes preparatory exercises and gently leads into Yoga Nidra. This makes the long variation quite time consuming. If you do not have the time to do the entire long variation, you can do just Shavyatra every day.

Yoga Nidra and Sleep

Those who do this practice infrequently, when tired or at the end of the day, risk falling asleep. Do not fall asleep in this practice since you are developing a bad habit. This practice is meant to awaken you to a higher level of consciousness and not to put you to sleep. Some practitioners use Yoga Nidra to fall asleep. This misunderstanding is common since the practice means Yogic Sleep. However, Yoga Nidra is conscious rest and not unconscious sleep. Therefore, never use Yoga Nidra to fall asleep. If you are sleepy and are about to fall asleep, then speed up the practice and bring it to an end as soon as possible.

If you practice the long version of Yoga Nidra regularly, you may notice that the quality of your sleep improves and you need fewer hours of sleep. This does not mean that you do not need sleep at all. Interfering with the natural sleep patterns is unhealthy, even dangerous.

Yoga Nidra and the Three States of Consciousness

The technique of Yoga Nidra leads to the state of Yoga Nidra. There are three states of consciousness: waking, dreaming and deep sleep. Every night, when you go to bed, you go to the dream state. Almost everyone remembers some dream or the other, therefore you can relate to the dream state. However, every night you also go into deep sleep. In this state you do not dream. This is a state in which the mind and body rest. You do not know this because you do not have a recollection of this state. Through the technique of Yoga Nidra, if well prepared and done regularly, you can consciously experience this state of deep sleep. Thus, the unconscious experience of deep sleep is just deep sleep; the conscious experience of deep sleep is Yoga Nidra.

Q&A

Question: Is Yoga Nidra a technique or a state of consciousness?

Answer: The technique of Yoga Nidra and the state of Yoga Nidra are two different things. The technique is a set of instructions that anyone can follow mechanically. However, the technique may not necessarily lead you to Yoga Nidra, the state of conscious deep sleep. You may not be able to distinguish between the two initially, if you have not experienced conscious deep sleep, but once you have a glimpse of conscious deep sleep you will know the difference.

Question: It is possible to visualize the moon in this version of Yoga Nidra. What is the significance of the moon?

Answer: This variation of Yoga Nidra gives you the option of using one single object for visualization: the moon. We know the idea of the sun and moon and its relationship with the mind, the breath and the nadis. The moon is deeply connected to the creative feminine energies or the unconscious mind. The Ajna Chakra is the center of the waking state or the conscious mind, the Vishuddha Chakra is the center of the dreaming state or the active unconscious mind and the Anahata Chakra is the center of deep sleep or the latent unconscious mind. The active visualization of the moon at the Vishuddha Chakra can act as an aid in activating the unconscious mind. Allowing the image of the moon to emerge would be a finer and subtler practice than active visualization of the moon.

Question: Why does this version of Yoga Nidra have almost no visualization?

Answer: There are many different variations of Yoga Nidra in the different tantric traditions and these have been practiced over millennia. Sages and yogis wandering throughout India kept this technique secret. Most of these different variations have detailed visualization techniques.

Visualization practices keep the mind busy; the mind cannot rest. Visualization also means adding artificial lights, which distract the mind from the genuine light of prana.

There is almost no visualization in this version of Yoga Nidra. You are literally in the dark space of your mind and body, waiting for the inner light of consciousness to emerge. From a technical point of view, this is the simplest version requiring little or no visualization. However, some may perceive it as difficult because the mind is not kept perpetually busy.

Question: You mentioned that one should not fall asleep during Yoga Nidra, but I have heard that Yoga Nidra is an excellent practice for those with sleep disorders. I know of persons who practice Yoga Nidra just to fall asleep. Please comment.

Answer: This is a common misunderstanding since Yoga Nidra is often referred to as Yogic Sleep leading one to believe that it is a practice that helps one sleep. However, Yoga Nidra is a conscious state of rest; it is not the unconscious state of dreaming or deep sleep that we generally consider as sleep. It may well happen that the regular practice of Yoga Nidra improves the general quality of sleep, but Yoga Nidra should never be used to fall asleep.

Question: Some say that the technique of Yoga Nidra was invented in recent times by a teacher of a yoga school in India. Is this true?

Answer: The different techniques of Yoga Nidra are tantric practices and were developed over millennia by *tantrikas* of different lineages and traditions. Any authentic technique of Yoga Nidra was not invented by any one person; it developed through *shruti* or "revelation" and was validated by an entire lineage of teachers. Yoga Nidra is one of the most ancient practices and is the right of all humanity. The idea that any one person should have "invented" it, and has a special claim on it, is false.

Question: I have tried to practice the entire sequence of Shavyatra, Shitalikarana and Yoga Nidra and find that, instead of helping me relax, it makes me extremely restless. Am I doing something wrong?

Answer: It is not unusual that initially the practice of Shavyatra, Shitalikarana and Yoga Nidra in one uninterrupted session makes the practitioner feel restless. This is because most of us are not prepared for such deep practices. It is important to follow the 7 Step Program slowly and gradually without skipping over the basics. To master the advanced pranayama practices, it is essential to focus on a healthy and well balanced lifestyle. If you are experiencing restlessness in spite of systematic practice then there are two options.

The first option is to go back to the basics and spend more time with the breathing techniques, especially diaphragmatic breathing. Focus on breath elongation; allow the breath length to reach at least 20 counts inhalation as well as exhalation, before you try the long sequence of Yoga Nidra.

The second option is to practice and master Shavyatra first. Only when you are absolutely comfortable with Shavyatra should you add Shitalikarana. When you can comfortably practice both Shavyatra and Shitalikarana in a single session, then the state of Yoga Nidra will come naturally and effortlessly to you.

Question: Can I do Aum Kriya with the mantra Soham instead of the sound Aum?

Answer: The mantra Soham can be divided into two parts: "So" and "Ham." The mantra Aum, on the other hand, cannot be divided. The two syllables in the mantra Soham create a subtle pause in the breath; exhalation does not flow smoothly into inhalation and inhalation does not flow smoothly into exhalation. If you have not mastered the breath without pauses as explained in Sushumna Kriya (Fig. 6.5), then you may use the mantra Soham in Aum Kriya Variation 1 (Fig. 11.1) and Aum Kriya Variation 2

(Fig. 11.2). If you have mastered the breath without pause, then use the mantra Aum.

Do not practice Aum Kriya Variation 3 (Fig. 11.3) and Aum Kriya Variation 4 (Fig. 11.4), until you have mastered the breath without pause. When exhalation flows smoothly into inhalation and inhalation flows smoothly into exhalation without any pauses, then only the mantra Aum is recommended.

Question: The description of Shitalikarana (from Fig. 11.8 to 11.15) does not show the breath without pause. Am I to allow the exhalation to flow into the inhalation and the inhalation to flow into the exhalation so that there are no pauses?

Answer: Shitalikarana is a long practice with 21 steps. Since the technique is long, it is not possible for most practitioners to practice it daily. There are many fine details to learn and master. It is possible in the initial attempts that there are pauses in the breath. Therefore, it is best to memorize this technique first and learn to practice it correctly without external aids. When you have mastered the technique, you may focus on the finer details such as breathing without any pauses.

Question: We were always told that Shavasana is a relaxation exercise. How can it be a pranayama practice?

Answer: Shavasana is a simplified version of Shavyatra, the 61 points practice. Shavasana is generally given to those, who have trouble locating the points or to those, who do not have the concentration necessary to go through all the points.

Practices like Shavyatra energize the body and go very deep if done correctly over a long period of time. To master Shavyatra and experience it as pranayama, it is important to practice it daily and to change one's lifestyle. The power of attention awakens the subtle pranic energy, just as the power of attention opens sushumna.

Shavasana can also activate subtle energy if done correctly and daily over a long period of time. However, most practitioners are not well prepared with a change in lifestyle, food habits, etc., therefore, the practice of Shavasana remains superficial and helps relax the muscular system.

Earlier, these tantric practices were kept secret and revealed only to those who were prepared. Now that these practices are available to the general public, they have become relaxation exercises rather than pranayama practices. Even though, there are many benefits of practicing Shavasana for muscular relaxation, this highly sophisticated practice has become superficial.

Question: On practicing 61 points I had a strange experience. I felt as though my leg was being pulled. The experience was very intense. Can you explain this? Should I stop this practice?

Answer: Shavyatra or 61 points is a deep acting pranayama practice. If done correctly, it removes the blockages in the energy channels and the subtle energy in the body begins to flow. What you experienced was the movement of prana in the legs, perhaps even a removal of a blockage in the pranic channels. This was a direct experience of prana itself. It may not have been pleasant because it was unexpected and unusual. Once the pranic blockages are released and the subtle energy starts flowing freely, you will experience prana as beautiful and soothing. That you had such an intense experience is a sign of progress. You need not be afraid and you should definitely not stop the practice.

Question: I have great difficulty locating each of my toes when I practice Shavyatra. It seems that all my toes are one large lump and it is impossible to locate them individually in the mind's eye. Please advise.

Answer: This is a common issue for practitioners. It is difficult to activate the prana in the individual toes and that is why you do not have conscious control over each individual toe like you have over your fingers. The solution to this is daily practice over a long, uninterrupted period of time. Eventually, you will be able to locate each of your toes and over time you may also have conscious control over each of them, just as you do with the fingers of your hand.

Question: Can I use audio guides for pranayama practice?

Answer: If you should find an authentic audio guide, you may use it for a couple of times, just to get a feel of the technique.

Audio guides can be useful, but they also encourage dependency. If you keep using the audio guide, you will form a habit and find it difficult to do the technique without it. The audio guide will keep you at the external and physical level. With an audio guide you can never explore the depths of the practice and master pranayama. To master pranayama you will have to let go all external aids. It is best to memorize the technique and then drop all external aids. Initially, you may make mistakes. Go back to the book, reread it and correct yourself. After a couple of sessions, you will master the technique. Once you have mastered the technique, you will go deeper into the practice, naturally and effortlessly.

Question: Whenever I practice 61 points, at point 4 my mind completely wanders off. This happens every time. I seem to get lost in a train of thoughts, memories and fantasies instead of paying attention to the points. When my awareness returns to the body again, it is already time to stop the session. I feel discouraged by this. It seems I cannot do this practice. What would you advise?

Answer: This experience of the mind wandering off at a particular point is not unique to you. In fact, it is very common among practitioners. This means you have a blockage in that area. In your case, it is at point 4, the right elbow. While you may never know why you have the blockage there, you can work to release this blockage by continuing to do this practice.

As you approach the blockage, speed up the practice so that you do not really stop at the point. Do not skip the point; instead just touch upon it briefly. Crossing this blockage every time will give you confidence and motivate you to continue the journey through the body. As you continue, it is possible, you may encounter another such point. Now you know what you have to do: just cross over the point quickly. Over time the blockages will release. You may experience this release at an emotional level as well.

Question: Is Yoga Nidra a pranayama practice or an advanced form of meditation?

Answer: In the state of Yoga Nidra, the question "Who am I?" is answered through direct experience. You are the shining light of Pure Consciousness.

The technique of Yoga Nidra as well as all the other practices outlined here in this chapter are pranayama practices; as you attain mastery in these, they lead you to a higher state of consciousness. The external world seems to disappear. The dream world also seems to disappear. In deep sleep there are no more objects. There is only the subject, the one, who witnesses.

If you have systematically gone through the program as outlined in this book you may have noticed that some of the practices seem to merge as you keep practicing them over a period of time. It seems that all the practices lead to one and the same place. This is a very good sign that reveals great progress on the part of the practitioner. At this point the question, whether Yoga Nidra is pranayama or dhyana, becomes irrelevant.

Chapter 12

REVERSAL OF SUBTLE ENERGY OR KUNDALINI AWAKENING

Are you upside down? Or is the world topsy turvy? The death of ignorance is the birth of wisdom. An adept, a mystic, a seer is born. All the same, awakening the kundalini is not the same as leading it consciously.

We are already familiar with the seven main chakras located along the spine, from the base of the spine to the crown of the head. Yet we do not know the exact nature of the chakras. In this chapter, you will get a glimpse into the true nature of chakras.

Even though there is extreme heat in the desert, you cannot cook an egg in a pan by holding it out in the sun. This is because the energy of the sun is not concentrated enough to cook the egg. It is scattered. Similarly, the energy in the body is generally scattered or diffuse, but in the chakras, the energy is densely concentrated. The chakras are the wheels of life.

Nadis and Chakras

The nadis run throughout the body transporting energy to the different parts. In certain areas of the body there are large intersections of these channels. These intersections are the chakras. The chakras are nothing other than energy hubs (Fig. 12.1).

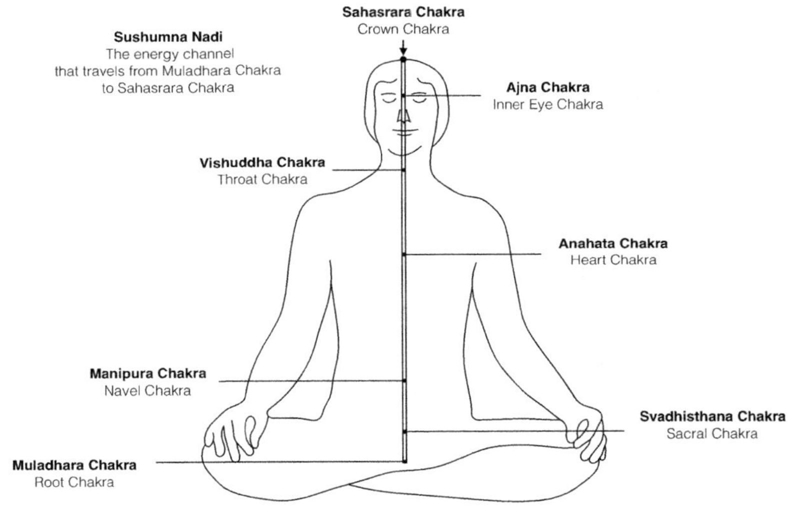

Figure 12.1 **Chakras and Sushumna Nadi**

Consider the traffic that runs on the highway network throughout a country. Since important cities must be better connected, they have more highways connecting them to other important cities or facilities like airports and railway stations. The energy channels in our body connecting the important organs are like highways running throughout the country. The more important the organs, the larger the energy channels emerging from them as well as nourishing them. The most important organs are along sushumna, the central energy highway of the body. The limbs, for instance, do not have energy highways or important nadis, but smaller nadis that sustain them. Interestingly, the chakras correspond with the important plexus or network of nerves. The Muladhara Chakra corresponds to the pelvic plexus. The Svadhisthana Chakra corresponds to the hypogastric plexus. The Manipura Chakra and the Anahata Chakra correspond to the solar plexus and the cardiac plexus respectively. The Vishuddha Chakra corresponds to the pharyngeal plexus and the Ajna Chakra corresponds to the nasociliary plexus.

If one of the important highway junctions is closed due to an accident or construction work, the traffic system in the entire country does not collapse and come to a standstill. Instead, the traffic is diverted to alternative routes and in spite of the disturbance and the inconvenience caused, it continues to flow. Similarly, a blocked chakra will not kill you, but the blockage may affect the overall health of the body.

The subtle yogic body and its energy channels were mapped through yogic intuition and through practices such as Shavyatra. The actual mapping of the physical human body had never been done until the human body was dissected. European doctors in colonial India, who had already dissected the body, were amused by the idea of chakras and nadis since they had not located these in the body. It should be understood that nadis are not shiny blue and silver nerves running through the body; they are subtle energy channels.

Electric wires carry electricity, but the electricity itself remains invisible to the eye. The presence of electricity can nevertheless be felt when you experience an electric shock. It can also be deduced through a well functioning electric gadget. Cutting open the body and looking at the nerves does not mean you can see the subtle energy channels, the nadis. The presence of the invisible pranic energy is felt in well functioning organs and a healthy mind and body. A disturbance in the flow of energy can be experienced as disease and poor health. The European medical community was only familiar with the gross form of the body. European doctors were looking for lotuses, triangles and other geometrically shaped objects, because they did not understand their significance. The diagrams of nadis and chakras with lotuses and geometrical figures found in ancient scriptures are merely symbolic representations of subtle energies.

The chakras and nadis were mapped in a healthy body using yogic intuition and pranayama practices. If you practice in a systematic way, then you too will be able to map the energy field in your own body. When you are able to do this, you can find the blockages in your body and learn to remove these. Since the body is an intricately connected field of energy, a blockage in one area can affect another seemingly unconnected area.

Nadis and chakras form a blueprint of the body. Just as information stored in computers can be copied and transferred to another computer, the nadis and chakras manifest a new body in the next birth. If the original file of a computer is damaged, the copy on the new computer will also be damaged. Similarly, if the fine and subtle energy field of the body is damaged due to an unnatural death or surgery, this can impact the body in the next life. Dissecting the body meant damaging the subtle pranic energy, this is why dissection was taboo. The same was true for surgery. This is also why all traditions of the world have similar death rituals of keeping the body until the prana has left completely. To declare the person clinically dead is not sufficient from a pranic point of view. Death is a process of separation of prana from the body, leaving behind only dead matter. This process can take several days. This is why traditionally bodies were kept for up to ten days and longer, before being cremated or buried.

Manipura Chakra and Agni Sara

The Manipura Chakra is the largest of the chakras since the maximum number of nadis flow through this chakra. If this chakra is completely open and energy is flowing freely, then the body remains healthy. One practice that opens this chakra is *Agni Sara*.

Agni Sara is a kriya of tantric origin and is therefore not a commonly known practice. *Agni*, like a lot of Sanskrit words, has many meanings. *Agni* means "fire" or "energy." Agni is also used with reference to the sun. *Sara* means "lake." Agni Sara energizes the entire solar system of the body or in modern terms the solar plexus. This practice activates the vast reservoir of energy in the body.

How to practice Agni Sara

Stand with your feet about 15 cm apart. Bend the knees and simultaneously bend from the hips to place the palms of your hands on the knees. Rest the weight of the upper body through your arms just above your knees. While leaning forward, keep the back straight and do not bend your head. You may close your eyes; this will help you focus and locate the right muscles (Fig. 12.2).

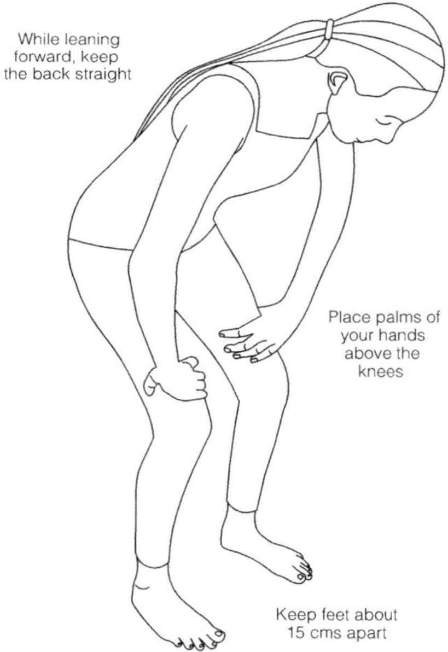

Figure 12.2 **Agni Sara**

To do Agni Sara correctly, it must be well coordinated with the breathing. Exhale and contract the muscles in the lower abdomen just above the pelvis. Pull them in and up. As you slowly inhale, gently release the abdominal muscles, allowing the lower abdomen to return to its natural position. This is 1 round. It is important to pull the abdominal muscles in and up and eventually let them move down and out in a circular movement. It is not a difficult practice, but many have difficulty in locating the muscles in the lower abdomen.

Guiding Principle

When the abdomen and chest are compressed in any posture, exhale. When the abdomen and chest are expanded in any posture, then inhale.

Diaphragmatic breathing will lead you to Agni Sara, but with a difference. In diaphragmatic breathing you exhale and relax. Exhalation is a passive process. The inhalation, on the other hand, is active. Agni Sara is the opposite. In Agni Sara, you actively exhale, while you pull in your abdomen and then you inhale, as you relax.

Agni Sara is always done in standing position. It may be done in seated position if you have a physical handicap or cannot stand due to weakness or obesity. Agni Sara should not be practiced by pregnant and menstruating women.

Mastering Agni Sara: 7 Month Plan

Agni Sara is one of the finest pranayama practices and it churns up the energy in the body. Agni Sara activates the Manipura Chakra and the entire network of pranic channels. It also facilitates the removal of pranic blockages. You can do up to 140 rounds of Agni Sara daily. However, it is best to start gradually. One of the greatest masters of this practice was Sant Gyaneshvar, a thirteenth century tantric master. Wandering mendicants were able to access this storehouse of internal energy so that they could cope with the bitter North Indian winter.

If you have never done Agni Sara, begin by doing 20 rounds a day. It might be difficult to do all the 20 rounds at once; instead do 5 rounds spread out over 4 sessions. You can increase the rounds by 5 per session each month (Table 12.1). In 7 months you should be able to do Agni Sara 140 times a day. If you do it more than 100 times a day correctly, you will have perfect digestion and become very efficient in any field.

Month	4 times a day	2 times a day	Once a day
1	4 x 5	2 x 10	20
2	4 x 10	2 x 20	40
3	4 x 15	2 x 30	60
4	4 x 20	2 x 40	80
5	4 x 25	2 x 50	100
6	4 x 30	2 x 60	120
7	4 x 35	2 x 70	140

Table 12.1 **Agni Sara – 7 Month Plan**

Granthis or Knots

There are three main *granthis*. The word *granthi* has different meanings. It means a "doubt" or a "knot that is tied tightly and difficult to undo." Granthis are blockages in the nadis. There are three main blockages in the pranic channels.

Rudra Granthi

The first granthi is in the region of Muladhara Chakra and the Svadhisthana Chakra. The direction of the energy flow is outward into the world and downward from the Sahasrara Chakra to the Muladhara Chakra. The practitioner does not have a contemplative mind and the tendency to be externally oriented is very strong. The very first obstacle is turning the direction of the energy inward and upward from the Muladhara Chakra to the Sahasrara Chakra. The reversal of energy flow is extremely difficult. This granthi is the one that makes sure that the worldly activities do not cease. It is at this granthi that the world illusion is maintained. Cutting through this granthi means beginning the process of dissolution (Nivritti Marga) and changing the energy flow from outward and downward to inward and upward.

Vishnu Granthi

The second granthi is in the region of the Anahata Chakra. The Anahata Chakra is central and it is here that the downward traveling and the upward traveling energies of the body are balanced.

Brahma Granthi

The third granthi is in the region of Vishuddha and Ajna Chakra. The Ajna Chakra is the most mysterious of all chakras and the gatekeeper of the mystical chakras beyond. Cutting through this granthi releases immense amounts of energy; it completely and radically changes the way you perceive the world. The opening of this chakra makes a mystic of an ordinary person. Suddenly you discover: what you considered to be life is in fact dull and lifeless and that, which you considered to be death is eternal life. Seen from this perspective, cutting through the Brahma Granthi leads to a kind of rebirth. Such a person is called twice born.

Understanding the Granthis

Each granthi seems like an unsurmountable obstacle to the practitioner and it is difficult to say which granthi is the toughest to cut through. The first granthi is probably the most difficult to cut through, because it means a complete change of perspective or an absolute reversal of the energy flow from outward to inward and from downward to upward.

Having pierced the Rudra Granthi, the largest of chakras, the Manipura Chakra must be opened. With the help of Agni Sara a reservoir of energy is accumulated and *Uddiyana Bandha* is applied to regulate and cut through the Vishnu Granthi.

Cutting through the granthi at the Ajna Chakra releases tremendous amounts of energy and completely changes the way you see the world. Crossing this knot heralds the birth of a mystic and seer. However, cutting through the last knot is not the end of the journey; it is, in fact, the beginning. The one who has destroyed the world illusion and has a glimpse of the eternal now longs to be established in the highest of chakras, the Sahasrara Chakra, the thousand-petaled lotus.

Bandhas and the Reversal of Energy

Ida and pingala are rivers of energy that flow downward from the crown of the head to the base of the spine. This downward flow dissipates the energy. You want to reverse the flow of energy by opening the sushumna nadi and taking the energy upward to its source in the Sahasrara Chakra through the central channel.

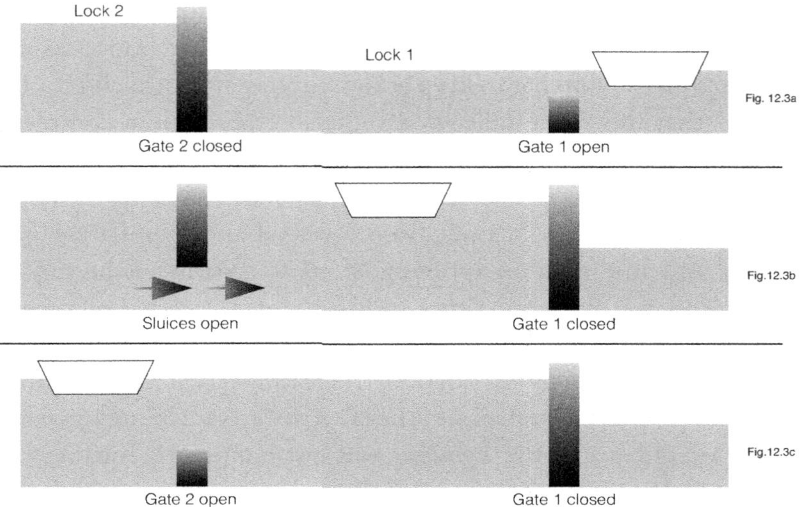

Figure 12.3 **Canal Locks**

Imagine you are in a ship that comes in from the open sea and starts its journey up the river. This river is in a mountainous region and you want to go upstream as well as uphill since there is a difference in altitude. While it is possible to go against the flow of the river upstream, it is not possible for a ship to go upstream as well as uphill. To do this, the ship requires a system of canal locks. These can be seen on many rivers throughout the world.

The boat or ship enters Lock 1 (Fig. 12.3a).

The boat goes right to the end of Lock 1. Gate 1 is closed. Gate 2 remains shut but the sluices are opened or water is pumped in. This increases the water level and the ship rises (Fig. 12.3b).

Now the water level in Lock 1 and Lock 2 is the same. Gate 2 is opened while Gate 1 remains closed. The ship goes over to Lock 2 and is at a significantly higher altitude (Fig. 12.3c).

Pranayama, the science of prana, includes mastery of the bandhas and mudras. If you wish to raise the energy from the Muladhara Chakra to the Sahasrara Chakra, then you must learn when to apply the three yogic locks. Imagine, there is no altitude difference and the river is just meandering through the plains, yet, there are locks on the river and the ship has to keep going through the locks. It is quite obvious that this is a totally meaningless exercise and a complete waste of time. This is what happens when you practice *bandhas* before sushumna has been opened and the energy starts traveling upward.

If the energy flow has not been reversed and is not traveling upward and you insist on applying *bandhas*, then in the best case, you are just wasting your time, and in the worse case, you create more obstacles for yourself. Do not practice the *bandhas* forcefully or based on external recommendation. The *bandhas* will happen naturally when sushumna opens and the energy starts traveling upward. If you are not ready, the *bandhas* will not happen. It means you need to continue to prepare yourself systematically with changes in lifestyle, diet, etc. Do not get impatient.

With a great deal of effort and practice you change the flow of energy and it starts flowing upward, but you find it almost impossible to take the energy right to the Sahasrara Chakra directly. It is now that you need a *bandha* to act like a canal lock and stop the energy from flowing downward again. The word *bandha* has many different meanings such as: "a lock," "to bind," "to tie," "to join," "to dam up" or "to create an embankment."

There are three important yogic bandhas:

Mula Bandha, the Root Lock

The Root Lock is called so, because it helps to pierce the Rudra Granthi at Muladhara Chakra. Mula Bandha stops the dissipation of energy into the external world and prepares the mind to turn inward. It is like a dam that stops the outward flow of energy. The energy flow starts to reverse and goes upward and inward instead of downward and outward. If the practitioner has not prepared himself with change in lifestyle, diet, etc., the forceful application of techniques is unlikely to reverse the flow of energy.

Uddiyana Bandha, the Upward Flying Lock

Uddiyana means "flying upward." When the energy starts rising, it must cut through the Vishnu Granthi at the Anahata Chakra. The Uddiyana Bandha holds the energy here and regulates it, so that all the nadis are flooded with energy and the blocks released.

Uddiyana Bandha can be practiced in seated or standing position. As the energy starts rising, the body acquires its own wisdom and knows which position is appropriated.

In the standing position, bend forward and rest your hands on the knees, keeping the back straight. Exhale completely and pull the abdominal muscles completely in, creating a deep cavity in the abdomen. This is Uddiyana Bandha. If sushumna has been opened, then this is not just a contraction of muscles, but involves the regulation of subtle energy.

The Upward Flying Lock can also be performed in the meditative postures if necessary. The *Jalandhara* Bandha or the Chin Lock is applied simultaneously or immediately after.

Jalandhara Bandha, the Chin Lock

Jalandhara is a composite of two words: *Jala* means "water" and *dhara* means "a current." To perform the Chin Lock, bend the head and place the chin in the hollow of the throat. This is the easiest of the bandhas.

How the Bandhas work

The bandhas can also be seen as base camps on the way to the top, to rest and gather the energy before taking on the next phase of the climb.

The Mula Bandha prevents the energy from moving downward and being dissipated. The Uddiyana Bandha gathers and holds a huge reservoir of energy to cut through Vishnu Granthi and Rudra

Granthi. Once the Vishnu Granthi has been pierced, the energy must be harnessed and its use regulated. This flood of energy from the Manipura Chakra must be regulated into a strong current that is capable of piercing the last of the granthis. The function of the Jalandhara Bandha is to regulate this flow and lead it to and through the Ajna Chakra cutting through the last of all knots.

When the energy flow is redirected upward, the bandhas are applied naturally and effortlessly. For instance, when you prepare yourself well with changes in lifestyle and diet as well as practice daily, the energy flow reverses and Mula Bandha happens spontaneously and naturally.

Mudras

The word *mudra* has many different meanings, such as "seal" or "closing." While there are many academic as well as intellectual interpretations, the Oral Tradition interprets this as sealing or closing the energy circuits to prevent the energy from being dissipated. Thus, mudras are subtle energy circuits; they are much subtler than the bandhas.

You are already aware that you have positive and negative energy from the right and left sides, that is, pingala and ida respectively. When the energy circuits are open, the energy does not flow. As one progresses in pranayama, these energy circuits close naturally to allow energy to flow freely.

To understand how these subtle energy circuits function, you must know that the energy flow is categorized according to its qualities. The different fingers of the hand are connected to these qualities (Fig. 12.4):

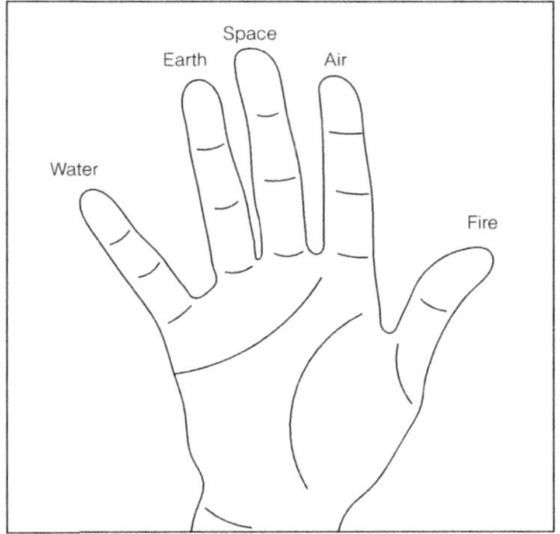

Figure 12.4 **5 Elements**

- The thumb is agni or fire.
- The forefinger is vayu or air.
- The middle finger is *akasha* or "space."
- The ring finger is *prithvi* or "earth."
- The little finger is jala or water.

Anjali Mudra

A well known mudra that everyone knows and uses for prayer is *Anjali* Mudra. *Anjali* means "reverence" or "benediction." In this mudra you hold the palms of your hands together; the two thumbs come together, the forefingers touch each other, the middle finger touches the other middle finger, the ring fingers touch each other as do both the little fingers. When all ten fingers are joined together, all the fine energy circuits are closed and subtle energy can flow.

Jnana Mudra

You are already familiar with Jnana Mudra. After Anjali Mudra this is the most commonly practiced mudra. It is also known as *Chit* Mudra. *Chit* means "consciousness." Thus Chit Mudra is the seal of consciousness. In this mudra, agni (fire) and vayu (air) come together. Since a fire blazes only in the presence of air, one can well imagine that this mudra ignites and sustains a great deal of subtle energy.

Other Mudras

There are many different kinds of mudras: Dhyana Mudra, *Avahani* Mudra, *Dhenu* Mudra, *Matsya* Mudra, *Yoni* Mudra, *Kurma* Mudra, *Shunya* Mudra, etc. You do not need to learn all these mudras.

The energy that flows on applying mudras is so fine and subtle that most people do not feel it. That is why it is not necessary to do all sorts of mudras. When the energy starts flowing in sushumna, the bandhas follow naturally and so do the mudras. You may start doing different mudras, even though you may have never encountered or learned them before.

Awakening and Leading Kundalini

The entire process of pranayama is about mastering and regulating the energy potential of the body. One learns to stop the outward and downward dissipation of energy, turns the flow of the energies inward and upward and learns to awaken the kundalini. The process begins with simple breathing exercises and eventually leads to advanced pranayama practices. These pranayama practices, including bandhas, seek to reverse the flow of energy. Irrespective of the number of breathing exercises and pranayama practices you do, do not expect this reversal of energy to take place if there are no changes in lifestyle including food habits.

Awakening kundalini on its own is not really a sign of significant progress. Awakening kundalini means you get some insights into the nature of the mind and life but it is not sustainable. Until the practitioner has pierced the Ajna Chakra, he does not attain the higher states of consciousness. Mastery means awakening and leading kundalini upward, piercing the chakras and the granthis and leading kundalini back again to "Her own Abode," the Svadhisthana Chakra.

Q&A

Question: Why does one have to lead kundalini back to Svadhisthana Chakra, "Her own Abode?"

Answer: Leading kundalini from the Muladhara Chakra to the Sahasrara Chakra is the inward path known as Nivritti Marga. Such a practitioner is at home in the higher levels of consciousness; he is a mystic with little interest in mundane matters. Leading kundalini back to Svadhisthana Chakra is Pravritti Marga, the outward path.

The complete path is called Purna Marga; it is the higher path because you gain mastery in the inward as well as the outward paths. This means the adept retains the mystical insights and wisdom for the benefit of humanity. The kundalini must be led back to Svadhisthana Chakra, so that the practitioner retains interest in serving humanity. If the practitioner does not know how to lead kundalini back to Her own Abode, then he remains established in the higher chakras and loses interest in worldly matters.

Question: Do all the pranayama practices regulate the prana at the layer of energy known as Pranamaya Kosha?

Answer: Breathing exercises, being superficial, are regulated at the first two layers: the physical layer and the energy layer. Pranayama practices, on the other hand, are not regulated just at the layer of energy, but also at the deeper layers of the body: the mental layer, the layer of wisdom and the layer of joy and bliss.

Question: What is *Ashvini* Mudra?

Answer: *Ashvini* means "possessing horses" or "horse woman." Ashvini Mudra is practiced by contracting the anal muscles and pulling the anal sphincter upward. It is relatively easy to locate these muscles mentally. It can be practiced standing or sitting. It is not necessary to apply Ashvini Mudra more than 3–4 times daily.

It is possible that the yogis, who lived in harmony with nature observed the contraction of the anal muscles in horses. However, the name also has a deeper significance. *Ashvin* also means "a horse tamer." The horse is an ancient and universal symbol of the mind. Like the horse, the mind is fast and powerful. A horse tamer, in this case, is one who can train and tame the mind. The Ashvini twins, the physicians of the gods, are also portrayed with horse heads, indicating that physical health is related to the mind.

The practice of Ashvini Mudra, although different from the classical hand mudras, is still a practice to seal the energy circuits and prevent dissipation of energy into the sensory world.

Ashvini Mudra is a good preparation for Mula Bandha since it helps to tame the outward moving energies of the mind.

Question: What is Mula Bandha and how do I apply it?

Answer: There is a proliferation of theories about where and how Mula Bandha is to be applied. The main reason for this is that Mula Bandha comes from an ancient science, but the modern student is seeking parallels in modern medicine with its emphasis on the human anatomy.

The most common theory is that Mula Bandha is associated with the center of the perineum. In men, Mula Bandha is said to be applied by contracting the muscles surrounding the perineal body, which lies midway between the anus and the genitals. In Siddhasana, pressure applied by sitting on the heel of one foot is said to stimulate contraction. In women, Mula Bandha is said to be applied differently. The contraction of Mula Bandha is apparently felt, not at the perineal body, but at the area surrounding the base of the cervix.

Located at the lowermost portion of the uterus, the cervix is a cylinder-shaped neck of tissue that connects the vagina and uterus. While men may apply Mula Bandha externally with pressure on the perineum, it seems women must learn to locate the cervix mentally to apply Mula Bandha. For both, men as well as women, the greatest difficulty would be to contract the isolated muscles.

The second theory is that Ashvini Mudra and Mula Bandha are the same. This is a misconception. Ashvini Mudra is applied by contracting the anal muscles and pulling the anal sphincter upward. These muscles are relatively easy to isolate and contract.

There is still a third possibility to explore. The study of ancient texts suggests that the application of Mula Bandha is at the Muladhara Chakra which is located at the base of the spine in the sacrococcygeal region. If this is the case, then Mula Bandha must be applied mentally by both genders.

All the above possibilities try to understand the Mula Bandha in the context of the human anatomy, forgetting that pranayama is an empirical science based on practice and observation. It is not necessary to focus on Muladhara Chakra or practice some technique of Mula Bandha; instead focus on the reversal of energy flow through changes in lifestyle and systematically mastering the fundamentals. The most important aspect of this process of energy reversal is training the senses. When the energy flow reverses, Mula Bandha is applied naturally and effortlessly. The program outlined in *Mastering Pranayama* prepares you for the reversal of energy flow, however Ashvini Mudra, Sushumna Kriya, Sandhya Kriya and Shavyatra can be emphasized to facilitate this process.

Question: Is Agni Sara the same as Uddiyana Bandha?

Answer: Agni Sara is completely different from the Uddiyana Bandha and it is important not to confuse the two. Agni Sara helps to activate the energy, which leads to the application of the Uddiyana Bandha and eventually to piercing through Vishnu Granthi. Agni Sara churns up the energy while Uddiyana Bandha regulates and directs it.

Question: I find it difficult to practice Agni Sara. It is difficult to locate the exact muscles that I am to pull inward and upward and then outward and downward. Please advise.

Answer: It is not unusual that you are having difficulty locating the exact muscles in the lower abdominal regions. This is because most of us are very tense and the abdominal muscles are "frozen." To train these muscles, practice diaphragmatic breathing. Diaphragmatic breathing leads to Agni Sara. Uddiyana Bandha too is an excellent preparation for Agni Sara. In this case, Uddiyana Bandha would work only at the muscular level and not act in its function as a bandha.

Question: What is the difference between bandhas and mudras?

Answer: Mudras close the energy circuits, so that prana starts flowing. Mudras are external, such as the different hand positions. Bandhas on the other hand are internal; they "dam up" the energy and redirect its flow.

The bandhas can be compared to dams that stop the water flow, redirect the river and generate energy. Mudras are like separate streams that are linked together to facilitate greater water flow.

Question: I was taught to apply the bandhas as part of the asana practice. Can I continue to do these?

Answer: Asanas are beneficial for physical health in many different ways. However, asanas cannot reverse the energy flow and lead it inward and upward. You need to take into consideration all the factors mentioned in Chapter 8 to reverse the energy flow. If the energy is not moving upward, it does not help to apply the yogic locks. If you apply bandhas before the energy starts moving, then it is only a muscular exercise and a massage for the abdominal area and no longer a pranayama practice.

You may practice Uddiyana Bandha as a preparatory exercise for Agni Sara. However, it is best to practice it individually and not in combination with asanas.

Question: I have heard references to a pranic bath or shower. Please elaborate.

Answer: The pranic bath is known as *abhisheka*. The word *abhisheka* means "anointment," "coronation," or "ablution." Abhisheka or the pranic bath is experienced naturally when the practitioner pierces the Brahma Granthi and comes in touch with the two secret chakras beyond Ajna Chakra and is eventually led to the Sahasrara Chakra. The second birth is experienced as an internal shower of energy from Sahasrara Chakra. It is accompanied by a pleasant change in the biochemistry of the body, that is felt acutely by the practitioner. The abhisheka is the highest attainment of an adept.

This internal pranic experience is enacted as a ritual bathing or a ceremonial sprinkling of water on the head in traditions all over the world.

Question: I have heard that there are five different kinds of prana called Apana, Udana, Samana, Vyana and Prana. What role do these have to play in the process of mastering pranayama?

Answer: There is only one undivided prana, but it has been categorized according to its functions in the body. In this context, they are referred to as Prana Vayu or simply Vayu. Vayu or air also means "winds of the body."

Apana Vayu is related to functions such as elimination and reproduction. *Udana* Vayu governs the higher functions such as speech, effort and evolution of consciousness. *Samana* Vayu governs digestion of food and impressions in the mind. *Vyana* Vayu governs circulation and movement.

The five vayus are regulated in the Pranamaya Kosha and are vital for the health and well-being of the body. The detailed study of the vayus in Ayurveda is interesting from a therapeutic perspective. Far more important for the purpose of mastering pranayama is to understand the difference between breath, prana, kundalini and shakti.

Chapter 13

LEADING KUNDALINI

In any other book, this would be the end, but in this book, it is a new beginning. The harnessed kundalini brings with it the unlimited power of the deep unconscious and the knowledge of life, the world and everything.

Breath, prana, kundalini and shakti are all forms of energy, yet, they are different. Understanding the subtle difference between these is critical to the process of mastering pranayama. This understanding is not meant to be an intellectual understanding. On the contrary, the sages have always emphasized the importance of direct experience or "seeing."

The breath is a gross form of prana. It is also known as vayu. Breath is merely air, while the nature of prana is consciousness itself. You can fill a balloon with air but that does not make the balloon a living being. Since breath and prana are different, breathing exercises and pranayama are also different.

Breathing exercises are superficial and relate to respiration. Breathing exercises can neither open the central energy channel sushumna nor reverse and lead the energy flow upward. They cannot lead to natural and effortless Kevala Kumbhaka.

Pranayama, on the other hand, is much deeper than breathing exercises. It uses awareness to regulate the energy flow in the body. With pranayama, the central channel can be opened, the energy flow can be reversed and the energy can be led upward. Kumbhaka occurs naturally and effortlessly.

Kundalini is also called Adi Prana

While prana is a more general term for the energy pervading the body, kundalini is a more specific form of prana. Prana is diffused and scattered through the body, like the heat of the sun in the desert. Kundalini, on the other hand, is concentrated and focused energy. It is like the heat of the sun that is focused with the help of a lens or mirror.

Kundalini is Adi Prana, the first unit of life. It has absolutely nothing to do with any modern yoga school or brand.

Kundalini is said to be sleeping at the Muladhara Chakra. The symbol of the kundalini is a snake, curled up and sleeping at the base of the spine. Just as diagrams representing the chakras are highly symbolic and there are no real lotuses and geometrical figures to be found in the body, similarly the snake too is symbolic. The snake is an ancient symbol to be found in all the traditions and societies of the world. The snake is full of the dark poison of emotions like desire, fear, greed, arrogance, selfishness, jealousy and anger.

Awakening the sleeping snake means coming in touch with the tremendous creative potential of the unconscious mind. Artists, writers, musicians and other creative people have unconsciously raised their kundalini and have access to the energy of the unconscious mind. Their kundalini is not resting at the Muladhara Chakra but at the Svadhisthana Chakra, "Her own Abode." Creative persons have access to the unconscious energy but only to a limited extent and not in a systematic manner. Creative persons who are unable to channelize this energy often suffer due to this.

The Wish-fulfilling Genie

Through pranayama and systematic meditation one can learn how to channelize the energy of the kundalini. This is not a simple task achieved by practicing a few techniques. It requires guidance, since raising the kundalini means to regulate the vast potential of the unconscious mind. One who raises the kundalini will come in touch with the language of symbols and the power of emotions.

While there is a great fascination for the power of kundalini, there is also a danger associated with this power. If you have not already learned how to navigate in the dangerous waters of thoughts, emotions, fears and desires, you can get lost. More often than not, the practitioner gets embroiled in all the thoughts, emotions, fears and desires that begin to surface, because he has not mastered the process going from the gross to the subtle.

The ancients tell a story of a king who had a genie. This genie could do anything, he could fulfill all the wishes and commands of the king. The only problem was that the genie always needed to be kept occupied. If he was not kept busy, he threatened to attack the king and devour him. The king found a lot of work for the genie. The genie built palaces, roads and temples for the kingdom until one day the king could no longer come up with work for him. As the genie chased the king wanting to devour him, the anxious king ran to his wise minister, seeking urgent counsel. The minister asked the genie to dig a hole in the ground and fix a long pole in it. He then told the genie, "When the king gives you work to do, then do the work and when he has no work for you, go up and down this pole." Thus, the wonderful works of the genie helped the kingdom to flourish and when he had nothing to do, the energies of the genie were channelized by traveling along the pole.

If you contemplate a little, you will recognize the deep symbols in this story. The kingdom is your body; and you, the body bearer, are the king. The wise minister is your inner wisdom and the genie is the unconscious mind or the incredible energy potential known as kundalini. This story gives a clue about how to train the unconscious mind. The pole is the sushumna nadi and letting the attention travel along the sushumna trains your genie, harnesses all his energy, so that he can do amazing things for you.

There are many such tales about wish fulfillment and they all relate to the incredible potentials of the unconscious mind. It should, however, be clear from this traditional tale that an untrained mind is a terrible monster that will devour you, as many brilliant creative minds have discovered. Kundalini, the sleeping snake, implies a great latent potential, but also a grave danger. While there is a fascination for kundalini, the question remains: If you would understand the true nature of kundalini, would you still want to awaken and lead the kundalini upward?

To harness the potential of the unconscious mind is no mean task. It requires great courage, stamina and determination. The great skill and science is learning to lead the energies inward and upward following the principle of reversal. Awakening the kundalini is only the beginning of the entire process. Learning to raise the kundalini is not enough, you must also learn to lead it back to Svadhisthana Chakra, "Her own Abode."

While breathing exercises are preliminary and preparatory in nature, pranayama is an attainment. Sushumna Kriya is one of the most important techniques to be mastered. Another important technique is learning how to shift the flow of the breath between the two nostrils without the use of Vishnu Mudra. Besides these two practices, elongation of the breath and elimination of the pauses in the breath are absolutely necessary for progress in pranayama.

If you practice systematically and have good guidance you will eventually learn how to harness all your energy potential. The sleeping serpent will awaken!

The Modern Word for Kundalini

Kundalini is not some esoteric eastern idea. Kundalini is an ancient word for the unconscious mind, or rather, the unconscious mind is a modern word for kundalini. While the sages knew and understood the power of the unconscious mind since millennia, modern science has started exploring and studying the nature of the mind and emotions only in the last few centuries.

The word kundalini is derived from the word *kundala* which means "coiled." A coiled rope or a coiled bracelet is also called kundala. To say that the energy is coiled, is to indicate that it is a form of potential or latent energy. It is visualized as a coiled serpent. It was observed that snakes rest in a coiled form and when they get active they uncoil themselves. The uncoiled energy is the potential of the unconscious mind. When the coiled snake that is at rest uncoils itself and starts moving, it is dangerous, but it is also dynamic.

To understand your own energy potential and learn how to harness it, we have drawn parallels with a modern form of energy: electricity. You experience electricity as you sit in the comfort of your homes, using modern devices and household gadgets. Our modern life would not function without electricity, yet few of us have been anywhere close to the source of power, such as a nuclear reactor. Nuclear energy is as close as it can get to a source of infinite power. Such power, in uncontrolled form, can lead to terrible destruction. The experience of Adi Prana is like being at the very core of a nuclear reactor. It is the source of infinite power. The first experiences of this power can be awe inspiring, even frightening.

While you have seen the benign side of electricity in your life, you also know of the terrible side of electricity in lightning. It is a very powerful and concentrated form of energy but completely uncontrollable; it can strike anywhere, anytime. Such is the nature of kundalini. Depending on the intensity and duration of the kundalini experience, it can completely overload the system. If you try to put a 12 voltage bulb into a 120 voltage fixture, the bulb is going to be destroyed. Your mind and body is like a 12 voltage bulb that is put into a 120 voltage fixture. You need to prepare your body and mind for such kind of high voltage power. Kundalini, in its raw form, is like lightening: powerful, unpredictable and uncontrollable. You must learn to lead this energy, that is, harness it.

Shakti: the Cosmic Breath

What awaits you if you harness this energy and are able to lead it upward consciously in a systematic approach? What awaits you if you learn how to charm the serpent and become its master? You find out through direct experience that just as the body is a field of energy, so is the world. Thus, prana permeates not just the body but the entire world. What modern sciences, such as physics, have discovered just a few decades ago was known to the ancient sages of India since millennia. The cosmic energy that pervades all of the universe and life is called shakti. While kundalini manifests in the body, shakti is non-specific and applies to energy in its unmanifest form. The practitioner sees that the world is made up of waves of energies. Shakti, it is said, is waves of energy.

The systematic practice of pranayama activates prana and specifically the kundalini. As we already know, kundalini is the power of the unconscious mind, and this means that sooner or later you will come in touch with the thoughts, emotions, fears and desires in the realm of the mind. A pranavadin would say that you have crossed the Ajna Chakra and are exploring the most secret of chakras that lie between Ajna Chakra and the Sahasrara Chakra. The practitioner experiences a great bliss as he expands to embrace all of humanity. He sees the world, nay the whole universe, as waves of bliss and beauty as he frolics in this Ocean of Consciousness. This is shakti. All is sacred and all is of divine origin.

All the rhythms of nature and the universe are manifestations of the cosmic breath. Your breath whispers the mantra "Ham" as it exhales. Your breath sings "Sa" as it inhales. This is *ajapajapa*, the eternal mantra Hamsa. Your body is a miniature universe. Know yourself and all will be known. Begin by listening to your breath. Your breath, the bridge to the eternal, will lead you within. Your own breath will lead you eventually to shakti, the cosmic breath. When you listen to the cosmic breath singing, you know the difference between breath, prana, kundalini and shakti.

APPENDIX

LIST OF ILLUSTRATIONS

LIST OF TABLES

USEFUL LINKS

Visit our educative website:
http://www.that-first.com

Follow Radhikaji:
https://www.facebook.com/radhika.shahgrouven

Join Facebook Group:
https://www.facebook.com/groups/THATfirst

ABOUT THE AUTHOR

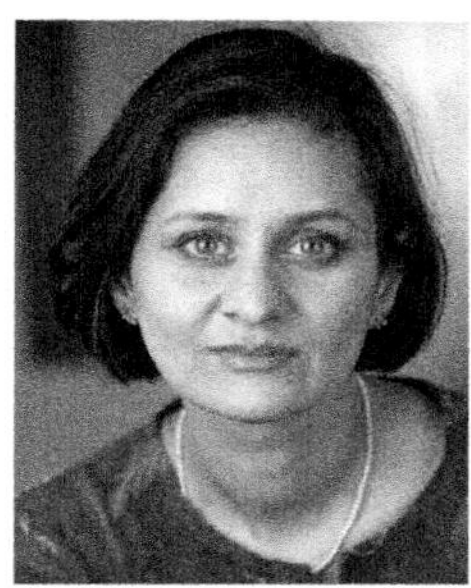

Radhika Shah Grouven is a teacher of Samaya Srividya. She has been teaching and writing on Yoga, Advaita and Samaya Srividya Tantra since 1992. She founded the organization THATfirst in 2009 to promote the authentic teachings of the Oral Tradition to students from different parts of the world. She leads retreats and gatherings in Germany and India. She regularly conducts online meetings that are available worldwide through www.that-first.com. She was born in Mumbai, India and is currently based in Germany.

PERSONAL NOTES

PERSONAL NOTES

PERSONAL NOTES

Printed in Great Britain
by Amazon